REILLY'S BATTERY

Captain H. J. Reilly,
5th U. S. Artillery,
Comdg Light Batt'y F, 5th Arty
Killed at Peking China, Aug 15th 1900.

Reilly's Battery
A Story of the Boxer Rebellion

MONRO MACCLOSKEY
BRIGADIER GENERAL, USAF (RET.)

RICHARDS ROSEN PRESS, INC., NEW YORK 10010

Standard Book Number: 8239-0145-9
Library of Congress Catalog Card Number: 69-19136

Published in 1969 by Richards Rosen Press, Inc.
29 East 21st Street, New York City, N.Y. 10010

Copyright 1969 by Monro MacCloskey

All rights reserved. No part of this book may be reproduced in any form without written permission from the publisher, except by a reviewer.

First Edition

Manufactured in the United States of America

DEDICATION

This book is dedicated to my father, Brigadier General Manus McCloskey, who began his distinguished career of forty years in the United States Army as a Second Lieutenant in Reilly's Battery.

ALSO BY MONRO MAC CLOSKEY

Your Future in the Air Force
How to Qualify for the Service Academies
Reserve Officers Training Corps
You and the Draft
NATO, Guardian of Peace and Security
The 885th Bomb Squadron (Heavy-Special) in World War II
Secret Air Missions
Pacts for Peace
The Infamous Wall of Berlin
The U.S. Air Force, Its Roles and Missions
The American Intelligence Community
From Gasbags to Spaceships
Hallowed Ground, Our National Cemeteries
Our National Attic
Alert the Fifth Force

About the Author

Brigadier General Monro MacCloskey, USAF (ret.), a command and jet pilot, began his career in 1920 as a West Point Cadet, graduating in 1924. Shortly after the outbreak of World War II, he was ordered to England as a member of the staff charged with organizing the 12th Air Force and planning the invasion of North Africa. He participated in the first assault landing in North Africa and later became Deputy to the Assistant Chief of Staff for Operations of the 12th Air Force, with headquarters in Algiers.

In the course of the war, General MacCloskey held a wide variety of posts, including those as Chief of Organization, Training and Equipping Section, Operations Division, Northwest African Air Force; a member of the Joint Planning Staff of the Mediterranean Air Command; and Assistant Director of Plans for the Mediterranean Allied Air Force. He organized, equipped, trained, and commanded the 885th Bomb Squadron (H) Special of the 15th Air Force, which engaged in the night dropping of resistance personnel and supplies into southern France, northern Italy, and the Balkans, and the 15th (later redesignated the 2641st) Special Group, which performed similar functions throughout Europe. In addition, General MacCloskey flew fifty combat missions.

After the war, General MacCloskey attended the National War College and upon graduation was appointed Chief of the Air Intelligence Policy Division at A.F. Headquarters. He served as Air Attaché to France, Belgium, and Luxembourg, and at the time of his retirement was Commander of the 28th Air Division, Air Defense Command.

His World War II decorations include the Silver Star; Legion of Merit with Cluster; Distinguished Flying Cross; Air Medal with seven Clusters; E.A.M.E. (Europe-Africa-Middle East) Medal with nine Stars and one Arrowhead; Army Commendation Medal with Cluster; two French Croix de Guerre with Palm and two with Gold Star; two French Legion of Honor, one Degree of Officer and one Degree of

Commander; Order of the Partisan Star; and Decoration of the Sultan of Morocco.

General MacCloskey is now the Executive Director of the Air Force Historical Foundation, with headquarters at Bolling Air Force Base, D.C. He is also a guest lecturer at the USAF Special Air Warfare School, Hurlburt Field, Florida.

Contents

Foreword   11

I.	Captain Henry J. Reilly	17
II.	Reilly's Battery in Cuba and the Philippines	22
III.	Rise of the Boxers	61
IV.	Forebodings in Peking	69
V.	The Besieged Legations	78
VI.	The Seymour Relief Expedition and the Taku Forts	89
VII.	The Capture of Tientsin	103
VIII.	The Peking Relief Expedition Takes Shape	118
IX.	Supply and Transport on the March	130
X.	The Relief of Peking and Paotingfu	139
XI.	Reilly's Battery in China	156
XII.	Epilogue	178

Appendix

I.	Proclamation by the Viceroy of Chihli	183
II.	Mr. Conger's Communications of June 3 and 4, 1900	186
III.	Joint Note of the Powers	188

Maps and Illustrations

Captain Henry J. Reilly	Frontispiece
The capture of Santiago, 1898	23
Map of the provinces of Cavite and Batangas	27
Operations map of General Grant's Brigade	28, 29
One of Captain Reilly's guns at Big Bend	32
Officers of the 4th Infantry and 5th Artillery at Imus, November 1899	34
Operations map of General Schwan's Brigade	38, 39
Officers in the Philippines, 1899	59

Plan of Peking	72
Lines of defense of the Legation Quarter	79
Route of Admiral Seymour's Relief Expedition	90
Route of the China Relief Expedition	141
A gun of Reilly's Battery in action in Peking	166
A page from Lieutenant McCloskey's diary	167
The Chien Men where Captain Reilly was killed	171
Lieutenant McCloskey and "Pet" in the Temple of Agriculture, Peking	172
Official announcement of Captain Reilly's death	174
Memorial to Captain Reilly in Arlington National Cemetery	176

Foreword

In putting down the Boxer Rebellion, the great antiforeign upheaval that shook China in 1900, U.S. Army and Navy forces played a vital role. As early as November 1898, in the face of the outbreak of violence against foreigners in China, Marine guards were established at the American Legation in Peking and the Consulate in Tientsin. These were withdrawn in March 1899, but worsening conditions required the reestablishment of the guard at Peking. In June, July, and August of 1900 this Marine guard fought valiantly, in concert with the troops guarding the other legations, against Chinese attacks on the foreign quarter in Peking.

When the Seymour Relief Expedition, which attempted to force its way from Tientsin to Peking, was turned back and itself besieged, it was obvious that strong military action had to be taken by the great powers to save the diplomatic representatives of eleven countries beleaguered in the legation quarter. U.S. Army and Navy forces, and troops of Great Britain, Japan, France, Germany, Russia, Austria, and Italy combined in an international move, the China Relief Expedition, to deliver the legations. *Reilly's Battery* was part of the U.S. forces in the operation, and it was his battery that won lasting fame when the thorite shells they fired opened the first gate into the Imperial City. As Captain Reilly stood on the wall above the Chien gate observing the fire of his guns, he was struck by a Chinese bullet and killed.

This book is the story of the Boxer uprising, the siege of the foreign legations in Peking, Admiral Seymour's unsuccessful Relief Expedition, and the successful China Relief Expedition in which Captain Henry J. Reilly's Light Battery F, Fifth Artillery, played such a gallant and historic role. There may still be alive in Peking today old men who as teen-agers wore the uniform of the Imperial Chinese Army or the Boxer trappings who, from behind barricades, fired away at the "foreign devils" who returned their fire and stubbornly refused to admit defeat. But there are few Americans alive today who participated in this epic expedition.

The diplomatic staffs of eleven countries were besieged in the legation quarter, but the troops of only eight countries participated in the successful relief expedition. Some of the individuals who survived the siege and a few of the military personnel with the relief expedition have written accounts of their personal experiences. Since there was no radio in 1899-1900, and the telegraph lines between Peking, Tientsin, Tangku, Taku, and intermediate points were destroyed early in the rebellion, the legations and relief forces had only vague information—which was sometimes wrong—as to each other's situation. Both, however, maintained some records of events that were written shortly after they occurred.

My father, the late Brigadier General Manus McCloskey, was a young second lieutenant, just graduated from West Point, when he joined Reilly's Battery in 1898. Much of the material in this book comes from his original handwritten diaries, letters to his fiancée who became my mother, and to his mother and father, and from the stories he told me over the years of the exploits of this remarkable organization. With the exception of the photograph of the gravesite of Captain Reilly, all photographs were taken from my father's personal collection. The original handwritten history of the battery, written by the battery's anonymous historian, was among my father's papers and was a source of great value. Official dispatches between State Department personnel, official communications between Army and Navy commanders, some of which are included in the Appendix, and numerous government records have also been used as source material for the book. Other sources are the private papers of government officials and military officers.

It should be explained that before going to West Point my father attended a business college where he learned it was easier to write McC than MacC, as in the family name. His application for admission to the U.S. Military Academy was signed "McCloskey," and that spelling, which continued the rest of his life, has required frequent explanation throughout the succeeding years.

In the preparation of this book I am indebted to the Department of State, the Library of Congress, the National Archives, the Army Library in the Pentagon, the Library of the Army and Navy Club of Washington, and the Palisades Branch of the D.C. Public Library. The U.S. Army Map Service was also extremely helpful by providing several of the maps and charts of the areas where Reilly's Battery was in action. I am most grateful to Mrs. Ann Clark, the Librarian of Bolling Air Force Base, and her staff for their valuable assistance in providing research materials. I also wish to give very special thanks to my sister, Sally MacCloskey, who spent many weeks reading all of

Foreword

Father's letters written from Cuba, the Philippines, and China, and marked all passages pertaining to Reilly's Battery. Her indexing and cataloging of the contents of the many letters was truly a labor of love and a tremendous help in writing the book.

For me personally the preparation of the manuscript has evoked many wonderful memories of my father. The thrill and excitement of the youthful, newly graduated West Pointer, as he served under an outstanding battery commander in such glamorous and faraway places as the Philippine Islands and China, are eloquently expressed in his letters. It is so easy to visualize Father dashing with his guns from position to position, supporting the infantry and firing away at the enemy.

From this portrait of Old China there emerges some understanding of the background to the clash between Chinese nationalism and the invasion of the foreign countries. This confrontation continues to have worldwide repercussions because it laid the foundation for Red China's present attitude toward foreign countries. The story of the historic achievements of Light Battery F, Fifth Artillery, in the Philippines and in China, under Captain Reilly's expert teaching and training, proves that "Leadership is always in style."

Monro MacCloskey

Washington, D.C.

REILLY'S BATTERY

Chapter I

Captain Henry J. Reilly

"These guns can go wherever cavalry can go."

Brigadier General William Montrose Graham, U.S. Army, is believed to have been the first artilleryman to make that statement, and, so far as is known, Captain Henry J. Reilly was the first to prove it. In Cuba, the Philippines, and China, Reilly's Light Battery F, Fifth Artillery, made infantrymen footsore with their rapid advances.

There is little to be learned about Captain Reilly and his men except by word of mouth and from personal war diaries. Correspondents did not follow artillery because the light artillery generally followed everything but transportation in an advance. Had not Reilly been struck by a Chinese bullet as he stood on the wall of Peking that bright morning in 1900, he would soon have completed his thirty-ninth year in the American Army and still have been a captain. He never had higher rank in the volunteers as had many of the regulars, nor had he ever had any staff duty assignments of record. Wherever his battery was, there was Reilly. Politics and a "pull" in Washington were unknown to him.

With all his hard work in the field, Reilly was frail physically. Lacking one inch of being six feet tall, he normally weighed only 145 pounds, and in the field his weight often was below 130. He was a neat, straight, soldierly man with steel-blue eyes behind pincenez, a high, intellectual forehead, and a mustache and close-trimmed beard streaked with the gray that came with thirty-nine years in the service. "Getting too thin for this business," he would say on the morning after a night's rest on the floor of a native hut. "My shoulder blades are about through."

"Thank you, McAuliffe." "You are very good, Protz"—or Smith, etc.—could be heard every few minutes wherever Reilly happened to be, for in courtesy he went nearly to extremes. Enlisted men who arranged his bunk, put up his tent, or brought him water, all in their line of duty, were sure of an expression of thanks. His men almost worshipped him. His orderly and trumpeter were two Germans who had enlisted years before and had been together in the battery for ten years. Protz was in his 50's, and Blonn was only a year or so younger. Each was close to six feet tall and thick and broad in proportion. Reilly's footsteps were dogged by one or the other of them on and off duty and, although they were bunkmates, there was a tinge of jealousy between the Germans as they vied to serve their captain. The proudest possession of each was a handsome silver matchbox, a treasured gift from Reilly on his return from Cuba. Protz' only complaint was: "De captain, he cuss us out; 'Lie down dere, lie down when under fire'—and *he* walk around without bending a knee."

F Battery's captain was a fatalist, as were many others who had had "taps" blown over their graves. "There's no use dodging," Reilly would say. "You will be hit when your body and bullets are at the same place at the same time, and that's the only rule there is to eighteen or twenty engagements without being wounded."

"But you have played your chances, haven't you, captain?" "Possibly, but I am now playing on those of some poor fellows who got it early in the game," he would reply. "But when I die, I want it to be in action."

When Reilly filled his battery in New York after returning from Cuba, he received fifty or sixty horses from what was known as the Yale Battery, a volunteer organization from the college. His own horse was a towering, rangy bay named "Sherman." He was a Kansan by birth, and his tireless energy showed that he had Jayhawker qualities. Reilly had bought him at Fort Riley, Kansas, and took him to Tampa, Cuba, Fort Hamilton (New York), San Francisco, Manila, and to China. There Sherman, his saddle now empty, was to follow his master's body to the grave as a good Army horse should. On a campaign, Sherman's walk was so fast that the mounts of the other officers had to canter or pace to keep up. Reilly and Sherman were a well-matched pair.

The captain had his own theories about the care of his men and the employment of artillery, and he put them into practice. Every man in the battery wore his khaki coat, rain or shine, and no matter how hot it was. They might leave off their shirts, or their very skins if they could, but the dun-colored blouse had to be worn so that the men might not become targets for native bullets. Despite the many engagements of Battery F, casualties were comparatively few, and Reilly believed this was largely due to the fact that the men's blue flannel shirts were covered. The battery also had a fine health record. In garrison or in camp all the water for the men was boiled before drinking, a refinement sometimes skipped in other outfits. But in Reilly's battery a court-martial was a certain consequence of disobedience to this rule.

Another "Reillyism" was that none except commissioned officers, and enough noncommissioned officers to protect the horses when they were taken to water, could carry revolvers. The recruit who had pictured himself comparisoned with an artillery saber (called more familiarly a "battle-axe") and a revolver was doomed to disappointment. The captain believed his men would be more efficient if they relied solely on their guns, without sabers, revolvers, or carbines. "What if your guns were attacked from ambush while the horses were attached?" he was asked one day when he was speaking of the unarmed men in his battery. "Our guns are never where they can't be brought into action," he replied and went on to explain his method. On the march in the enemy's country he had each gun attached to the ammunition box with a rope. In a moment the rope could be let out twenty feet, and the gun was ready for action, with the horses attached and moving. He often used this arrangement in the Filipino campaign.

During Brigadier General Theodore Schwan's expedition in the province of Cavite in the Philippines, Reilly's battery outdid even itself. Day after day it was in the advance, clearing the way with canister and shrapnel for the foot soldiers who followed. That Schwan's casualties were so light was largely due to the effectiveness of Reilly's guns.

To an infantryman, the recklessness of Reilly's men in driving their teams caused many a shudder. Down embankments into a morass of mud, water, and rank growth the heavy guns would be dragged, tilting and half falling. The six ambitious and eager horses would go plunging, snorting, and pitching, and drivers and gunners using whips tugged at bridles, straining and gasping, their faces black with slimy water. Reilly would be on the bank, certain that one more tug, all together, would bring the gun out and that he could save ten miles to and from a bridge that might be down. At times these feats cost horses, but nobody ever accused the captain of demanding the impossible of his artillery horses, which he cared for almost as much as he did his men.

While marching through Cavite below Imus, Reilly lost five horses in one day. One was wounded, but the others died of heat. They had recently arrived from the United States and had not become acclimated to the extreme heat and humidity. It was made the rule that all newly arrived horses from America would be kept in corrals for eight weeks before going into field service, and thereafter the artillery teams stood up well in the taxing climate.

Reilly was generous in giving his officers and his first sergeant opportunities to distinguish themselves. He had not forgotten that he himself had come up from the ranks. He had enlisted as a private in 1862 and won his commission for bravery in combat. His lieutenants, Summerall, Burgess, and McCloskey, were given every chance to make records for themselves. When they left Luzon for China, each had the distinction of a wound or two and a recommendation for promotion because of gallant conduct. At the New York horse show in 1898 when the battery was stationed at Fort Hamilton, it nearly monopolized the honors in the military tournament. A lieutenant was always in command, but Reilly was there every night, sitting in some obscure seat and wearing civilian clothing. Few spectators in the admiring audience knew that he had anything to do with making the battery the object of their applause.

When Light Battery F was ordered to the Philippines, Captain Reilly carefully selected his three lieutenants from the Fifth Artillery, and the three young men, all West Point graduates, were destined to serve him and their country with distinction. First Lieutenant Charles P. Summerall, class of 1892, became a famous commander of the First Division during World War I and later was Chief of Staff of the U.S. Army. First Lieutenant Louis Ray Burgess, also class of '92, commanded the Thirty-first Artillery Brigade in World War I. Burgess learned an immediate lesson when he was fighting the Filipinos near Imus in 1899. In violation of Reilly's orders he removed his khaki coat to assist the cannoneers in laying (aiming) their 3.2-inch gun against the insurgents. His blue flannel shirt made him more visible to the enemy, and he was shot in the leg between the ankle and the knee.

Twenty-four-year-old Second Lieutenant Manus McCloskey, who was to become my father some years later, had graduated in June of 1898, full of military theory and thrilled to be sent off to war almost immediately. Although he was to fight in many campaigns and serve under many brilliant leaders, and achieve the rank of brigadier general, he never met an officer he so loved, admired, and respected as Captain Reilly. His own career included many honors, and one of his picturesque comments in World War I has gone down in history. His command, the Twelfth Field Artillery, arrived near Château-Thierry to relieve an exhausted French regiment at a crucial point in the war. Under heavy shell fire and in view of the German observers in the positions just vacated by the French, he asked the French colonel for their firing data. The colonel protested vehemently. "It is madness. It is impossible to remain here. Surely you are going to retreat." "Retreat, hell," said Father, "we just got here!" No longer so young as when he served Captain Reilly, he still had the Battery F spirit and accomplished his objective. Even in his later years he loved to tell the tales of the excellence of "my Captain" and was never able to speak of Reilly's untimely death without fresh sorrow.

The captain was a man of parts. With all his soldiery severity, Captain Reilly knew how to live well in the field. Two Chinese servants made his mess one that provoked longing for invitations to dine with him in officers of other organizations with the expedition. Chicken was seldom lacking, although only these two Chinese knew where it came from, and they could disguise the ever-present rice into something delectable beyond recognition. At the table the officers wore their coats, brushed and buttoned, for the captain always did so, and they knew his standards. The meal was served and eaten with all the formality of an officers' dinner at the "spooniest" Army post in the States.

Captain Reilly, who was born in Ireland, had a wife, two daughters, and two sons back home, and was inordinately proud and fond of his family. He enjoyed golf and often talked of the game as relaxation after a day's march in Luzon. Among his fellow officers he was the man who drank what was to be drunk, but ended the evening as dignified and unruffled as when he first drew his chair up to the table.

"I expect to be in the Islands two years, when I ought to get a transfer home with my majority," he said on the Army transport on the way to Manila. His two years had not quite passed when he was killed. And so he died a captain, loved and mourned by his men.

Chapter II

Reilly's Battery in Cuba and the Philippines

Cuba had been one of the first Spanish colonies in the New World. Over the years the Spanish South American colonies had separated from the empire, and Cuba wished to follow their example. Cuban insurgents seeking independence were defeated in the savage Ten Years' War (1868-78). In 1895 Cuban patriots brought about a bloody revolution, provoked primarily by Spanish misrule and a sugar tariff. In an effort to put down the guerrilla activities, Spanish Governor General Valeriano Weyler inaugurated a "reconcentration" system in 1896. Under it Cuban peasants were uprooted from their lands and forced to live in towns occupied by Spanish troops, where many thousands died of starvation, disease, and exposure.

General Weyler's actions developed a strong pro-Cuban sentiment in the United States that was intensified by the heavy losses of American investments in Cuba and the publication of stories of Spanish barbarism. William Randolph Hearst's "yellow journalism" is often charged with inflaming public opinion. The insurgents refused a Spanish offer of autonomy and were determined to fight for independence. Demands for direct U.S. intervention began to circulate in America. The sinking of the U.S. battleship *Maine* in the Havana harbor with a loss of 264 men and 2 officers on February 15, 1898, further aroused war sentiment to fever pitch.

On March 9 Congress voted $50,000,000 for defense. On March 27 President William McKinley demanded that Spain grant an armistice for negotiation with Cuba and end reconcentration. On March 31 Spain offered to arbitrate the *Maine* settlement and end reconcentration, but felt that the Cubans should ask for an armistice. On April 9 Spain granted the armistice. But diplomacy was useless. Although Spanish complicity in the sinking of the *Maine* had not been proved, the public demanded that our national honor be avenged.

By April 10 President McKinley was aware that Spain had agreed

Reilly's Battery in Cuba and the Philippines 23

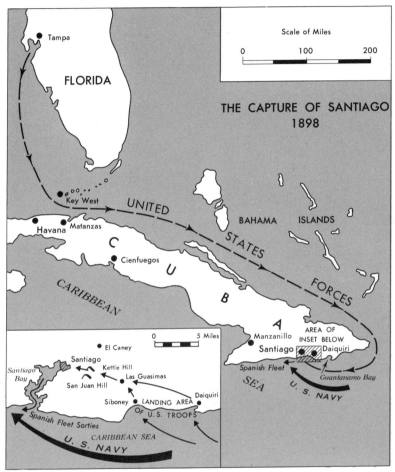

1. The capture of Santiago, 1898.

to every American request except the independence of Cuba. Yet on April 11, when he asked Congress for authority to intervene with military force in Cuba, he hardly mentioned this fact. Congress debated and then passed resolutions recognizing the independence of Cuba, demanding that Spain withdraw from Cuba, and empowering the President to enforce the demand. An Act of April 22 authorized the enlistment of volunteer troops. Spain declared war on the United States on April 24, and we responded by declaring a state of war had existed since April 21.

For once America was prepared for war. Commodore George

Dewey, who was in command of the Asiatic squadron, gave his famous order, "You may fire when ready, Gridley," in Manila Bay in the Philippines and sank the Spanish fleet there on May 1. On May 19 Spanish Admiral Pascual Cervera led the Spanish fleet in Cuba into Santiago harbor. When it attempted to escape on July 3, it was destroyed by ships commanded by Rear Admiral William Sampson and Commodore Winfield S. Schley.

In the meantime Major General William R. Shafter, with 16,654 poorly equipped but enthusiastic troops, had landed and begun a campaign to capture Santiago. The landings were made 15 miles east of Daiquiri and at Siboney on June 22. Included among the troops were the First U.S. Volunteer Cavalry, the "Rough Riders" recruited by Lieutenant Colonel Theodore ("Teddy") Roosevelt. Brigadier General H. W. Lawton and Brigadier General Adna R. Chaffee with 6,654 men attacked and captured El Caney, which was held by about 500 Spaniards. On that same day, July 1, Major General Joseph Wheeler and Brigadier General J.F. Kent carried San Juan Hill with 8,336 men. By July 2 Santiago was surrounded on its landward side, and on July 17 General José Toral surrendered to General Shafter in a ceremony outside Santiago. The Spanish flag was hauled down after a rule of 382 years. Major General Nelson A. Miles captured Puerto Rico July 25-28, and a few weeks later (August 12) the armistice was signed. The peace treaty was signed in Paris on December 10, thus ending the Spanish ownership of the lands discovered by Columbus.

The role of Reilly's Light Battery F, Fifth Artillery, in this complete victory was not a large one, but it did serve as their baptism of fire for some of the new men. Under telegraphic instructions from the War Department, Battery F, consisting of 4 officers and 75 men, fully armed and equipped, left Fort Riley, Kansas, on March 16, 1898, for Savannah, Georgia. The battery arrived at Tybee Island, Georgia, on March 19, where it was joined by Captain Henry J. Reilly, who had been on detached service at Fort Riley. It was to remain under his command—and gain its fame—until he was killed in Peking on August 15, 1900. The battery continued its southward movement from Chickamauga Park to Tampa, Florida, where it embarked on the transports *Comanche* and *Specialist* on July 3. The convoy passed Key West on July 4 and arrived at Altares on the 9th and at Baiquiria, Cuba, on the 10th, where the battery disembarked. They marched through Siboney the following morning and continued on to the front. They camped in the rear of General Chaffee's brigade, and during the night the gun pits were dug and the guns were placed in position before daylight on July 14. On July 18 the battery was moved to another position, and on the 22nd it was moved three miles inland near El Caney.

On August 11, Second Lieutenant Manus McCloskey reported to Captain Reilly and assumed command of the left platoon of Battery F while it was encamped near El Caney. The battery was bivouacked with others comprising the Light Battery Battalion commanded by Brigadier General Wallace F. Randolph, U.S. Volunteers. The troops all wore the very hot and very heavy American khaki, but the uniform of the artillerymen was trimmed with a red collar and red pocket lapels. The camp was in the foothills of a mountain range overlooking the valley in which lay Santiago de Cuba and the bay, with its tortuous inlet, and the rich tropical growth everywhere. This lush undergrowth was the hiding place of scorpions that had the habit of crawling into the toes of boots during the night and severely stinging their sleepy and unsuspecting victims as they dressed for reveille in the morning. It soon became standard practice to pound and shake the boots before putting them on.

On August 16 orders were received to break camp. Even while the battery was packing and preparing to march, buzzards watched and hovered over the camp waiting for the carcasses of the horses that had to be killed because they were unable to march. The coronary band at the top of the hoof would sometimes rot from standing in the heat and rain or lying in the soaked soil so that the whole hoof would fall off. It was a grim task for the men to shoot the horses they loved and cared for, but better than letting them live in such misery and suffering.

Around the outskirts of the camp, also anxious for the battery's departure, hovered a swarm of native Cubans, emaciated, half-clad, and pitiful to see, waiting to scavenge anything edible, wearable, or possibly useful that the battery might leave behind. The artillerymen marched into Santiago and bivouacked in the main street. Their ammunition was turned in to an arsenal and receipted for by a Spanish ordnance sergeant—an incident which seemed noteworthy.

On August 20 Lieutenants Newcomb and McCloskey, with about 70 men, embarked on the auxiliary cruiser *Resolute,* commanded by Captain Eaton, U.S. Navy. Captain Reilly remained in Cuba with the balance of the battery personnel, the guns, and horses, until embarking on the transport *Specialist.* To prevent bringing the Cuban yellow fever epidemic into the United States, the detachments of the battery were held in a detention camp at Montauk Point, Long Island, from September 3 to 19, when they moved by rail to Fort

Hamilton, New York. Here they were reunited as a battery under Captain Reilly. Lieutenant McCloskey was in command of the detachment that took part in the Military Athletic Tournament at Madison Square Garden (New York City) in March 1899, in which the unit won great public admiration with its skill in horsemanship as the battery's six-horse teams galloped through maneuvers and simulated going into action against the enemy.

On August 12, 1898, when the Spanish-American War armistice was signed, the city of Manila was taken by Admiral Dewey. The Cuban crisis had inspired a rising sentiment for independence in the Philippines that resulted in a violent revolt after the leader of the movement, José Rizal, was executed by the Spanish in 1896. The new leader, Emilio Aguinaldo, was fairly successful against the Spanish forces, and when the Spanish-American War began, the Filipino insurgents accepted American assistance. They reasoned that if America was planning to make Cuba free and independent, they, too, would be granted immediate independence. This, however, was not the intention of the United States. The Republic of Hawaii had been annexed in July 1898 at its own request, and Guam was acquired with Puerto Rico and the Philippines under the Treaty of Paris, with the United States paying Spain $20,000,000 for all its claim to the latter.

In anticipation of independence, Aguinaldo established a republic, naming himself as its president. After the fall of Manila he moved his government to Malolos to await the peace settlement between the United States and Spain. With the transfer of ownership of the Philippines to the United States under the Treaty of Paris (signed December 10, 1898), it was obvious that the independence of the Philippines was not to be granted. Aguinaldo and his 10,000 to 12,-000 Filipino insurgents began guerrilla warfare against the United States. They were not willing to trade Spanish despotism for American paternalism. So American troops were sent to the Philippines to put down the insurrection.

On April 3, 1899, Captain Reilly and Light Battery F left Fort Hamilton by rail, under War Department orders, for duty in the Philippines, arriving in San Francisco on April 10. Ten days later the officers and men, with the exception of a few drivers, embarked on the transport *Newport* for Manila. After stopping a few days in Honolulu, the transport arrived at Manila on May 23. The battery went into camp at Camp Otis and was attached to the First Division, Eighth Army Corps. The guns, horses, and battery equipment that had been sent on the steamer *Leelanaw* arrived in Manila and were unloaded on June 18, 19, and 20.

Operations in the Province of Cavite, Luzon, September 29 to October 8, 1899

On June 21, 1899, the battery left Manila and proceeded to the intrenched lines along Guadaloupe Ridge near San Pedro Macati. Two platoons under Captain Reilly were stationed at Haystack Knoll, and one platoon went to Telegraph Hill, about 3 miles away. Communication between the stations was by messenger, signal flag, and torch. The three platoons alternated in taking the position on Tele-

2. Map of Cavite and Batangas Provinces, Philippines.

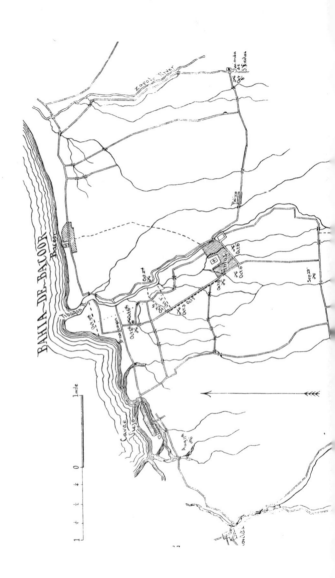

Reilly's Battery in Cuba and the Philippines

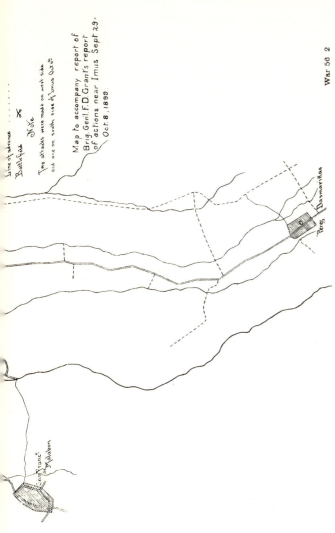

3.}
4.} Operations map of General Grant's Brigade.

graph Hill. The men called it "Camp Lonesome," and well named it was, too, for wood and water had to be carted by carabao (water buffalo) over almost impassable roads. Somehow in the distribution of rations, the Camp Lonesome platoon seemed to draw all the canned salmon, unpopularly known as "goldfish" and a further cause for griping. At Haystack Knoll there was a doubtful amenity—the men had plenty of literal "shower" baths. All they needed to do was add a little soap to the rainfall (47 inches in 30 days as measured in coffee cans).

During the time the battery was on this line, the horses were in Manila under the care of the drivers, and the guns, 3.2-inch caliber, were in pits on the line just in front of the men's tents. Drills were held daily, and special attention was given to the instruction of the gunners by the platoon commanders. It is safe to say that in the whole battery there were fewer than two dozen men who did not qualify as gunners and fuze-setters. This drill showed its worth in the fine gunnery of the battery later on and demonstrated again the wisdom of Captain Reilly.

On September 4 the battery left Guadaloupe Ridge and was assembled in the Cuartel Meisic in Manila, where it remained for a few days. The right platoon, consisting of 5 noncommissioned officers and 25 privates under command of Lieutenant Louis P. Burgess, left Manila and marched to Imus on September 6 for duty with Brigadier General F.D. Grant's Second Brigade, First Division, Eighth Army Corps. Three days later the platoon assisted in repelling an attack on an outpost at 11 P.M., firing canister and shrapnel. On the 10th Lieutenant Burgess, with one 3.2-inch gun, accompanied one company of scouts and two companies of infantry on a reconnaissance along Dasmariñas road. The enemy was discovered but not fired upon because orders directed that the enemy should not be engaged. Again on the 23rd, Lieutenant Burgess, with one gun, accompanied a reconnoitering party consisting of one battalion of the Fourth Infantry under Major Price along the Anabo road for 7 miles. These scouting parties found strong evidence of the gradual approach of the Filipino insurgents.

For some days prior to September 29 the insurgents had been assembling in the vicinity of the U.S. lines, which extended from Malibay along the seashore through Panañaque, Las Piñas (province of Manila), Zapote Bridge, Bacoor, and then up the Imus River to Imus in the province of Cavite, a total length of about 13 miles. Information had been received by the commander, General Grant, that about 1,000 insurgents under General Noriel had collected at Binang and Muntinlupa on the Laguna de Bay, that two regiments

—each about 1,000 strong—under General Alvarez had gathered at Silang and Dasmariñas, and that about 1,500 under General Trias were at San Francisco de Malabon and Noveleta. Silang, Dasmariñas, Malabon, and Noveleta are all in the province of Cavite.

On September 29 a scouting party, composed of one battalion of the Fourth U.S. Infantry, Captain E.H. Brown commanding; one 3.2-inch gun of Light Battery F, Lieutenant Burgess commanding; and the scouts of the Fourth Infantry, Lieutenant F. Guy Knabenshue commanding, was attacked by what was believed to be two battalions of insurgents at the junction of Malabon and Dasmariñas roads. The fight had lasted about one hour when the insurgents withdrew. Among the artillerymen only the wheel-driver of the leading gun was wounded in the knee by enemy fire.

The left platoon of Reilly's battery, consisting of 5 noncommissioned officers, 1 cook, and 18 privates, Lieutenant Charles P. Summerall commanding, left Cuartel Meisic with its guns on September 7 and proceeded by cascoe (a long, almost rectangular barge or lighter, sometimes with sails) to Calamba, reporting to Brigadier General Kline's brigade. Here Lieutenant Summerall relieved a platoon of Battery E, First Artillery, and took charge of two 1.65 Hotchkiss guns manned by a detachment of the Twenty-first Infantry. Summerall's platoon engaged the enemy's outposts on the 14th and 20th and again on the 22nd. On the 28th, 7 horses and 4 mules rejoined the platoon at Calamba.

The center platoon with battery headquarters, Captain Reilly, and Lieutenant McCloskey marched from Manila to Bacoor, about 13 miles south of Manila, on September 13 for duty with General Grant's brigade.

On October 1 General Grant received information that the insurgent forces had moved from San Francisco de Malabon and Noveleta into Cavite Viejo and Binacayan; from Silang and Dasmariñas to the south side of Imus (with a strong outpost at Palico); and from Muntinlupa and Binang to San Nicolas and Alamausa. On the morning of October 2 the telegraph line between Bacoor and Imus was cut. It was repaired but soon cut again. Strong patrols were then sent out from both Imus and Bacoor. Both patrols had more or less skirmishing until they reached Big Bend in the Imus River, about 1½ miles from Imus, where they found the insurgents strongly intrenched in a commanding position on the west side of the river.

The center platoon, with Lieutenant McCloskey commanding under the direction of Captain Reilly, received its first real baptism of fire on October 2 while stationed at Bacoor with the brigade

5. *One of Captain Reilly's guns at Big Bend. Lieutenant McCloskey (with field glasses) directs the firing.*

headquarters and a battalion of the Fourteenth Infantry. The platoon had marched along the Imus River at 5:30 A.M. to ascertain if the enemy were building intrenchments along the banks, but no indications were observed, and the platoon returned to its quarters. At about 10 o'clock that same morning the insurgents opened up a fire from the opposite bank of the Imus. Call to arms sounded and the platoon set off at a gallop and was soon at the scene of action.

Company F, Fourteenth Infantry, was in skirmish order along the road following the river and the center platoon was posted on its right. Captain Reilly rode along the line under heavy fire and directed Lieutenant McCloskey to open up on the enemy intrenched on the opposite bank near a group of nipa huts. By indirect fire, having previously made a road map of this locality, Lieutenant McCloskey burst shrapnel over the enemy and silenced their fire in that direction. The infantry then advanced, and Captain Reilly ordered the lieutenant to leave one gun, the 4th section piece, under Sergeant George Winniger, at the first position to protect Bacoor, and to bring the 3rd section gun along with the infantry, firing whenever deemed advisable. Shrapnel, shell, and canister were fired at ranges from 50 to 800 yards.

About noon Captain Eldridge, commanding Company H, Fourteenth Infantry, received orders to move his men along the road to effect a junction with the troops from Imus. Lieutenant McCloskey, with one section, accompanied him. This road followed the Imus River very closely, and the gun was marched on the road, taking advantage of clumps of bamboo for cover. The fighting was resumed, and the infantry and the section moved along the road together, covering each other's advance by their fire. At Big Bend the insurgents had constructed a trench and earthwork on the far bank and had a clear field of fire on the road used by the U.S. troops. Here the junction was made with the Fourth Infantry, and the enemy's fire temporarily ceased.

During the lull in the fight Captain Reilly, Captain Eldridge, and Lieutenant Glidden were standing in the open arranging the extension of the Imus troops to the Binacayan ferry and the contracting of the Bacoor line to hold the road open. Suddenly the enemy reopened with a murderous fire from the trench just across the river and not more than 50 yards away. Captain Eldridge fell, fatally wounded. Captain Reilly's better judgment conquered his wonderful courage, and, it is believed for the first time in his life, he dodged bullets. Musician Protz dropped to the ground as though shot and prudently sought the security of a friendly gutter.

The infantry and the gun of the section replied to the enemy fire. The gun was loaded behind a clump of bamboo, quickly run out, aimed, fired, and then drawn back to cover under sharp enemy fire. The gunner, however, was unable to find the earthwork, so Lieutenant McCloskey took over his duty and sent a zero shrapnel through the trench and cleared Big Bend.

During this fighting an infantry sergeant called to Lieutenant McCloskey, "Don't fire—there's a corporal out there. We've been trying

6. Officers of the Fourth Infantry and Fifth Artillery at Imus, November, 1899. (1) Major B. D. Price, Commanding; (2) Captain F. B. Andrus, Quartermaster; (3) Lieutenant Burgess, Fifth Artillery (wounded); (4) Lieutenant McCloskey, Fifth Artillery.

to get him out for a half hour but the enemy won't let us." There on the bank was the body of an infantry corporal, but in the middle of his forehead was a red spot where an enemy bullet had hit him. Seeing this, Lieutenant McCloskey sadly told the sergeant, "My gun will never wake that man; only Gabriel's trumpet can do that now."

General Grant stated in his report of the day's operations: "A section of the Fifth Artillery, under Captain Reilly, rendered excellent service during the day in driving the insurgents out of their intrenchments. I have no knowledge of the losses sustained by the enemy, but two men crossed the river after the insurgents left. On their return they reported counting 28 dead natives and that many were killed by the artillery."

On October 3 General Grant's troops began operations to thoroughly clear out the insurgents on the Binacayan side of the Imus River. At 9 A.M. Captain Reilly directed Lieutenant McCloskey to place his platoon in position to cover the ferrying of the troops from Bacoor. Heavy firing broke out on the Imus road. The 3rd section, with McCloskey commanding, advanced along the road as on the preceding day, firing canister and shrapnel at the insurgents above the ferry, and going into action again at Big Bend, now found to be more strongly held than the day before. The firing there was maintained in support of the advance of U.S. infantry troops. The enemy's fire was silenced, and the insurgents were driven from their position. The center platoon then marched on to Imus where Lieutenant McCloskey turned over command to First Sergeant Bertram Follinsby.

In the meantime this same day, Major Butler Price, commanding the Fourth Infantry, had not complied with General Grant's directive to sweep the west bank of the Imus River, but instead had sent Lieutenant Burgess with one gun, the scouts, and a battalion, north on the Binacayan road under the command of Captain Hollis, Fourth Infantry. This move was feebly executed, and sharp resistance was encountered at the second bridge on the Binacayan road. The column succeeded in taking the bridge just as General Grant arrived at Imus. In this encounter the right platoon, under Lieutenant Burgess, was engaged with the enemy at a range of 500 yards. The first gun, commanded by Sergeant Patton, and the second gun, under Sergeant Proctor, assisted in repulsing an attack on the outpost and clearing the enemy trenches on the Imus-Zinacayan road. In the fighting one horse was killed, and Lieutenant Burgess was seriously wounded in the leg. Lieutenant McCloskey then assumed command of the right platoon.

The left platoon under Lieutenant Summerall, with one 1.65 Hotchkiss gun, was likewise engaged with the enemy and, with the infantry and artillery, successfully repelled an insurgent attack on Calamba. That evening at about 5:30 a number of shots were heard from the west side of the river about half a mile south of Bacoor. A nearby patrol pointed out two shacks to Captain Reilly and said shots had been coming from them for the past hour. Under Captain Reilly's direction Sergeant Follinsby fired a couple of shrapnel into these buildings with such effect that the enemy firing ceased, and four Filipino insurgents were seen running away from the buildings.

The platoons of the battery at this time were "horsed" and "muled," two mules being leaders and two horses being wheelers, due to the fact that of the magnificent lot of 100 horses belonging to the battery at Fort Hamilton, only 24 were allowed to be taken to Manila. The mules behaved nobly, however, seeming very proud of their red artillery saddle blankets and brass-trimmed harness. The horses, who at first had seemed to feel a little put down, gradually became accustomed to the mules' being in front of them. In the frequent attacks on Imus, ordinarily one piece, unhorsed, was left at an outpost while the other gun with 6 or 8 animals, horses and mules, was taken from place to place on the outskirts of town as the enemy's attacks required. The roads were almost impassable: Six or 8 animals could barely move at a trot. Both the horses and the mules had a strong aversion to water in their ears. A number of times the animals had to swim across the Imus. If a drop of water got in a mule's ear, he would roll on his side and stop swimming so that he had to be towed across. If water got in a horse's ear, he would shake his head and swim so fast that the soldier with him could not keep up and would have to hang on to the horse's tail and be towed ashore. The men's language was exceedingly colorful on such occasions.

On October 4, Lieutenant McCloskey and the right platoon, with the second piece, accompanied a battalion of the Fourth Infantry on a reconnaissance to Binacayan from Imus. On October 6 the platoon was engaged in repulsing an attack on Imus, firing shell and shrapnel at the enemy in and beyond a fringe of bamboo about 400 yards from an outpost. The same day the left platoon shelled a sugar mill occupied by the enemy at Calamba, while the accurate and effective fire of the center platoon under Sergeant Follinsby materially assisted an infantry command in an engagement with the insurgents and in the capture of Binacayan.

On October 6 Captain Reilly brought the center platoon, under Sergeant Follinsby, from Bacoor to Imus where it rejoined Lieutenant McCloskey's platoon, and he assumed command of both platoons to participate in Brigadier General Theodore Schwan's expedition into the province of Cavite. The platoons marched to Binacayan where they drew four days' rations and forage. Reserve ammunition was carried on bull carts in the general supply trains.

Operations in the Province of Cavite, Luzon, October 7-14, 1899

At 9 A.M. on October 8 the platoons broke park and took their place in the column, the right platoon with the advance guard in rear of two companies of the Fourteenth Infantry. The center platoon was with the main body, the Thirteenth Infantry, in compliance with the following directives:

HEADQUARTERS SECOND PROVISIONAL BRIGADE
FIRST DIVISION, EIGHTH ARMY CORPS,
Binacayan, P. I., October 7, 1899.

1. The following organizations having reported in compliance with instructions from the department commander, will constitute a provisional brigade: Thirteenth Infantry, 11 companies, Colonel Bisbee commanding; Fourteenth Infantry, 3 companies, Captain Taylor commanding; Captain Tate's Troop, Third Cavalry (mounted), Captain McGrath's Troop, Fourth Cavalry (dismounted); two platoons Light Battery F, Fifth Artillery, Captain Reilly; Captain Shunk's Company Engineers; Captain Lowe's Scouts.

2. First Lieutenant Fred W. Sladen, Fourth Infantry, is detailed and announced as acting assistant adjutant-general.

By command of Brigadier-General Schwan:

FRED W. SLADEN,
First Lieutenant, Fourth Infantry, Acting Assistant Adjutant-General.

HEADQUARTERS SECOND PROVISIONAL BRIGADE
FIELD ORDERS,⎫   FIRST DIVISION, EIGHTH ARMY CORPS
No. 2   ⎭   October 8, 1899

1. This command will move out on the road to Cavite Viejo at 10 o'clock this morning.

It will observe the following rules and orders of march:

1. Captain Lowe's Company of Scouts; Troop G, Fourth Cavalry; 2 companies Fourteenth Infantry; 1 platoon of artillery, will constitute the advance guard. A detachment of the engineer company, consisting of 2 noncommissioned officers and 15 men, will march with the reserve, and will be under the engineer officer of the brigade. The requisite tools will be carried on a cart. Upon arrival in camp the advance guard will immediately establish the outposts.

2. The main body will consist of the Thirteenth Infantry, 1 company Fourteenth Infantry, the company of engineers, 1 platoon of artillery.

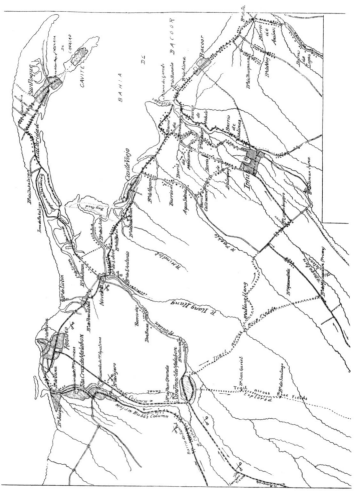

7.}
8.} *Operations map of General Schwan's Brigade.*

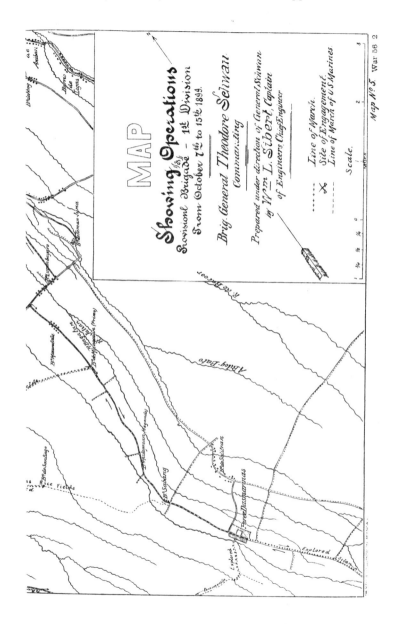

The commanding officer Thirteenth Infantry will throw out flanking parties to protect the flanks of the main body.

3. The train following the main body will be under the direction of the brigade quartermaster (Captain Biddle, Fourteenth Infantry). Its order of march will be: Ambulances, ammunition carts, and supply train.

The rear guard will be composed of Captain Tate's Troop, Third Cavalry; a detachment from it will protect exposed flanks of the train.

The above disposition for each day's march will be conformed to unless otherwise directed.

4. When passing through towns officers will see that men do not fall out of ranks. They will not detach men from their respective companies without absolute necessity.

By order of Brigadier-General Schwan:

FRED W. SLADEN,
First Lieutenant, Fourth Infantry, Acting Assistant Adjutant-General

The objective of General Schwan's expedition into Cavite was to punish and, if possible, destroy or break up the insurgent forces in the province—which had recently shown considerable activity in attacking the U.S. lines on both sides of the Tibagan River from Imus northward to Bacoor and Parañaque.

The strength of the insurgent troops in the municipalities of Cavite Viejo, Noveleta, Rosario, Santa Cruz, and San Francisco de Malabon had been previously reported by General Grant to be not less than 2,000. He had also estimated the enemy's force south of Imus as far as Silang at about 1,500. The latter force was to be held in check by General Grant's troops. The towns had heretofore been in possession of the enemy, and the hostile troops in the territory comprising these towns were designated as the primary objectives of the expedition. Depending upon the success of the movement as far as San Francisco de Malabon and across the difficult country northeast of it, the plan was to flank the enemy's forces menacing Imus or to attack them from their rear.

As a result of the reconnaissance operations of his command, General Grant stated that there were formidable enemy intrenchments between Cavite Viejo and Noveleta beginning at Putol, and that the entire road from that point to San Francisco de Malabon was protected by a succession of rifle pits and breastworks. He also stated that Rosario was extensively fortified on the sea side. General Grant expressed the opinion that the expulsion of the enemy from this locality would enable his troops to sweep the insurgents out of the province of Cavite, and that thereafter a comparatively small military force would be adequate to preserve the peace.

On October 7 General Schwan and the commander of the First Division, Eighth Army Corps, Major General H.W. Lawton, went by steam launch to Bacoor. From there they went to the barrio (a village or rural community unit) of Binacayan, two miles away, and located on the left bank near the mouth of the Tibigan River, which they crossed in a banca, a kind of canoe. That afternoon, Lieutenant Colonel G.F. Elliot, U.S. Marine Corps, commanding the marine battalion at Cavite Naval Station, called on General Schwan, offering on behalf of the Commander in Chief, U.S. Naval Forces on Asiatic Station, to move with a battalion of marines over the El Caridad causeway on Noveleta at the same time that General Schwan's column advanced on Noveleta from Cavite Viejo. The time for commencing the simultaneous movement was to be agreed on by the exchange of signals between the two bodies of troops. After a full discussion of the details the proposal was accepted, and the joint operation, which included the shelling of the beach by the gunboat *Petrel* preparatory to the advance of the marines, was successfully carried out.

The several organizations composing the expedition reported to Bacoor on the evening of October 7, and each was directed to march to Binacayan, the mounted troops, ambulances, and mule wagons crossing the river at Imus bridge, the foot troops and bull carts being ferried across. Considering the many difficulties that developed, the construction and operation of a ferry that consisted of a raft of four boats covered by a flooring that would provide sufficient roadway was effected very successfully and with remarkable dispatch by the company of engineers attached to the command. As fast as the west bank of the river was reached, the troops were bivouacked in the streets of Binacayan, which was occupied by a battalion of the Fourth Infantry of General Grant's command. Their outposts were withdrawn about 7 P.M. and were replaced by details from General Schwan's Provisional Brigade.

By the morning of October 8 all the organizations of the expedition had assembled at Binacayan. Their designations and effective strength were as follows on Table, page 42.

Under orders of the brigade commander, Captain McGrath, Fourth Cavalry, started with his own troop and Castner's company of scouts at 6:30 A.M. on October 8 to reconnoiter the road leading to Cavite Viejo. Finding that the enemy had evacuated the town, he immediately took steps to prepare it for defense. He also arrested some eighty natives whose appearance indicated their possible connection with the insurgents. Proceeding on the Noveleta road, the force

Organization	Commander	Effective Strength	
		Officers	Men
13th U.S. Infantry (11 companies)	Colonel W. H. Bisbee	21	1,022
14th U.S. Infantry (3 companies)	Captain Frank Taylor	4	263
3d U.S. Cavalry (1 troop)	Captain D. L. Tate	1	100
4th U.S. Cavalry (1 troop dismounted)	Captain H. L. McGrath Lieutenant S. A. Purviance	2	52
5th U.S. Artillery (Battery F, 2 platoons)	Captain H. J. Reilly	2	70
Lowe's Scouts (1 company)	Lieutenant J. C. Castner	2	63
Engineers (1 company made up from Co.'s A and B)	Lieutenant H. W. Stickle	1	120
Hospital Corps (detachment)	Major F. R. Keefer	7	26
Signal Corps (detachment)	Lieutenant W. L. Clarke	1	14
Total		41	1,730

made contact with the enemy's outposts, and shots were exchanged. A large enemy force was observed to be well intrenched in a position of natural strength.

The general topography of that part of Cavite Province through which the brigade conducted its campaign presented many difficulties. Generally speaking, all streams—most of which were hard to cross unless bridged—all the roads, and all separate properties were lined with almost impenetrable bamboo. Along the roads and near the habitations were additional screens of banana groves and other tropical plants. The bamboo screens were at various distances from the roads and occupied different positions with respect to them. There were nearly always such fringes practically parallel to the road and within the effective range of the Mauser, with other growths beyond, which further screened the enemy's movements.

The marching of the infantry was necessarily slow. All bamboo fringes from which the enemy could fire effectively had to be investigated by flanking parties, and in doing so the rice and cane fields and swamps had to be traversed. The flanking parties could not keep abreast of the troops on the roads, and frequent halts and changes of the flanking parties became necessary. The country was ideal for small ambushes and surprise attacks by an enterprising enemy acquainted with the terrain, and when enemy bullets were fired into a clump of bamboo trees they would bounce from tree to tree, making a terrific noise as though volleys were being fired.

The roads, however, were the most serious obstacles to quick and extended movements, especially during the latter part of the rainy season. Portions of the road were on low ground and these formed the beds of wet-weather streams. In these places the traffic of the country developed mudholes of such depth that it was necessary in several instances to hold up the heads of artillery horses that had fallen to prevent their being suffocated in the mud. Portions of the road that were high had no cross drains, and the seepage through the road beds at the natural depressions caused many temporarily impassable spots where the roads should have been good.

The general openness and difficult character of the rice fields south of the road made attempts to turn the enemy's right flank inadvisable. Accordingly General Schwan instructed Captain McGrath to examine the ground north of the road to determine the feasibility of a real or feigned attack on the enemy's left flank and detailed detachments from the scouts and his own troops for the purpose. They were deployed on both sides of the Bay road and soon drew the fire of the enemy, who were concealed in the brush covering swampy ground on each side of the road. When the reconnaissance showed that it was impracticable to attempt to turn the enemy's left flank, the order was given for an immediate frontal attack.

The main body of the expedition under Colonel Bisbee having arrived, a portion of its advance guard (E and G Companies, Fourteenth Infantry; Troop G, Fourth Cavalry; Castner's company of scouts, and one piece of artillery under Lieutenant McCloskey) was designated for this task under Captain McGrath. Three companies of the Thirteenth Infantry (B, D, and E), under Captain Saffold, and another field gun were sent to follow at a distance of 500 yards, with orders to support Captain McGrath's first line. The captain, moving forward at about 11 A.M., deployed Castner's company, supported by Company E, and Purviance's troop, supported by Company G, on the left and right sides of the Noveleta road.

On arrival at the outskirts of Cavite Viejo, Lieutenant McCloskey took the first piece of his platoon with the advance party of the vanguard, leaving the 2nd section piece in charge of Sergeant

Jay F. Proctor with the support. When the first line had advanced to the barrio Batamitan, about one mile from Cavite Viejo, it encountered enemy infantry fire from the front and flanks. The leading piece was brought to the line occupied by skirmishers, fired a few rounds, then advanced at a gallop, and fired again, in this manner keeping up with the infantry as it advanced by rushes. This continued until it came upon a ditch dug across the road to a depth of 5 feet and 8 feet wide, having 3 feet of water in it. The road on both sides was bordered by impassable rice fields where a field piece would have been hopelessly mired.

A few shots were fired over the advancing infantry troops, and when the enemy's fire lessened, the cannoneers began to fill up the ditch and make a roadway across it. The engineer troops under Captain Sibert came up shortly to assist, and as soon as the pieces and limbers could be drawn across by means of the prolonge, the platoon advanced. Captain McGrath, however, did not wait until Lieutenant McCloskey got his gun over the ditch; instead he pushed on. The Filipinos had an old smooth-bore gun of about 3-inch caliber hidden under the shack that covered the road of the advancing troops. They loaded it with iron nuts, bolts, pieces of lead, etc., and when it was fired Captain McGrath received one of the slugs in his thigh. He later died from its effects. Captain Saffold, Thirteenth Infantry, commanding the second line a short distance behind the first line, was also fatally wounded.

The enemy's intrenchments were well constructed on the far bank of the Rio Mindlot, with the stone bridge fortified and commanding the road over which the artillery had to advance. Sergeant Proctor's horse received a bullet wound in the neck, which he carried for two years without harmful results.

About noon the column resumed its march on Noveleta and, barring occasional ineffective shots fired by the enemy from the bamboo thickets along the road, arrived there without incident about 3:30 P.M. The two platoons of Reilly's battery went into camp at Noveleta, the guns of the right platoon being posted in battery at outposts nearest the enemy. The road that was to be traveled was impassable for some distance, and the enlisted men of the battery worked during the afternoon and evening preparing a new road. Upon entering the town the advance guard was fired upon from the houses; and throughout the afternoon and the greater part of the night the pickets kept up an irregular fire at the prowling insurgents. All the natives had fled, and, but for a few "Chinos" who refused to leave their stores, the place was deserted. A quantity of insurgent uniform cloth and a large amount of miscellaneous military supplies, such as insignia, flags, underclothing, made-up outer garments, shoes, etc., were burned by order of the brigade commander.

At Noveleta the vanguard of the brigade's advance guard communicated with scouts of Lieutenant Colonel G.F. Elliott's marine battalion of 20 officers and 356 men at a point about 500 yards from the village. The battalion had started about 10:45 A.M. when it heard heavy firing in the direction of Cavite Viejo. It pressed forward, driving the enemy from a small earthwork position that blocked the road, and inflicted some damage. The marines returned to their barracks at Cavite about 6 P.M., but their diversion probably drew off some troops from the enemy's intrenched position and protected the American right flank on its march to Noveleta.

Although the brigade arrived and bivouacked at Noveleta in good shape, some of its carts and wagons failed to do so. Due to the wretched condition of the road, many of them did not join their respective organizations until after midnight. The direct road from Noveleta to San Francisco de Malabon, to which the enemy was believed to have retreated, was reported as even worse and offered better opportunities for ambuscades than the miserable road just traversed. It was also found that while some of the troops were rationed until October 11, others had only enough subsistence to last them until the next day. General Schwan therefore abandoned his intention to go from Noveleta to San Francisco de Malabon and decided to carry out his original plan, which included Rosario and Santa Cruz in the list of places to be cleared of the enemy. Accordingly, instructions were telegraphed to Lieutenant Cunningham, who was in charge of the steam launch lying off Cavite Viejo loaded with supplies for the brigade, to proceed to Rosario.

On the following morning, October 9, the platoons of Reilly's battery broke park at 6 A.M., taking the same position in the column as on the previous day. As far as the central part of the barrio of Pasa Tabla the southern branch of the road leading to Rosario, although better than that farther north, was still indescribably bad. The flanking parties also had considerable difficulty penetrating the jungle along the roadside. As a result the march of the command was necessarily slow. After passing the barrio the road improved, but thereafter and until Rosario was reached there was almost constant firing by the advance guards at bands of insurgents hanging around its flanks and endeavoring to hinder its progress. The leading artillery gun was fired whenever any of the enemy was visible. While marching along a road covered with 20 to 30 inches of water, the leading piece struck a hidden obstacle, and the wheel horses were thrown off their feet. By strenuous exertion their driver kept the horses' heads above water and saved them from drowning, but in doing so he lost his haversack in the water. (Three months later it was found on the body of a dead insurgent at the fight at Putol Bridge.)

During this delay the second piece came up, a road was cut for it, and Captain Reilly ordered it up to take the place of the first piece at the head of the column, while he extricated the first piece from its mudhole. Meanwhile the flanking parties dragged many natives from their hiding places onto the road. Their terror-stricken faces substantiated the belief of their captors that although unarmed and clad in "amigo" apparel, they belonged to the hostile troops and had been firing on the Americans.

The column reached Rosario about 8 A.M. on the 9th, and the advance guard, which had been fighting its way into the town's outskirts, proceeded to make a thorough search of the place. Some 200 prisoners were arrested on suspicion and brought to the plaza. They all professed peaceful intentions and denied any connection with the insurgent army, so they were turned loose after the departure of the main column.

The towns of Rosario and Santa Cruz, both located on Manila Bay, lay on opposite sides of the Cañas River, an unfordable stream about 50 yards wide with its banks heavily fringed with bamboo. An iron bridge across the river about 1,500 yards above the Hacienda de Agustinos was supposedly held by the enemy. A detachment was sent at once to seize a ferry, or to occupy a ford by which it was reported that communication was maintained between the barrios of Julugan and Uana, the former being on the Santa Cruz side of the stream.

From the information obtainable, the mass of the enemy's troops were at or in the vicinity of San Francisco de Malabon, and a force variously estimated at from 600 to 1,000 had passed through the day before, or perhaps was still in Santa Cruz de Malabon. All reports agreed that a very considerable force, capable of operating on either or both sides of the river, confronted Schwan's brigade. If the command were to move directly on San Francisco de Malabon it would expose itself to the danger of an attack on the flank or rear from the Santa Cruz side. The insurgents' favorite tactic was to fight with a river between themselves and their opponents. Considering all factors, it was deemed best that part of the command should work up the left bank of the river, the principal column advancing up the other side.

Four companies of infantry, 27 engineer soldiers under Lieutenant Horton W. Stickle, one platoon of artillery commanded by Lieutenant McCloskey, and a few scouts and signal and hospital corpsmen were detached for this purpose. Major Jno. W. Bubb, Fourth Infantry, a veteran officer of considerable experience, was placed in command of the detachment. He was instructed to clear the left bank and the town of Santa Cruz of the enemy, keeping as nearly as possible abreast of the principal column and communicating with it by signal, or by means of the ferry, which he was to push up the river. Unless otherwise directed, he was to encamp on the river bank at a point opposite the Hacienda de Agustinos and then report for further instructions.

About the time of the column's arrival at Rosario, Lieutenant Cunningham's launch arrived and anchored off shore. Between the shore and the bar that extended all the way to Santa Cruz lay several hundred boats of a deep, narrow configuration with bamboo outriggers, about 40 of which were large enough to transport 35 men each. The remainder could carry from 15 to 22 men each. All the boats had masts and sails. The distance of the bar from the shore varied from 400 to 600 yards. Launches could not approach the shore closer than half a mile, and boats could cross the bar only at high tide. Cargoes of cascoes always had to be transferred at the bar to smaller craft or be carried to the shore by natives at low tide, when the water did not rise above their waists. Cascoes were used to transport the supplies from the launch to the bar, and natives were hired to carry them to the shore. Breastworks lined the beach all the way to Santa Cruz.

While the work of landing supplies was going on at the beach, Major Bubb was preparing his detachment for its special task. The right platoon, under Lieutenant McCloskey, joined the detachment at 1:30 P.M., marched to the Cañas River, and crossed it opposite the barrio Julugan near its mouth on a raft hastily constructed under Lieutenant Stickle's direction. The guns were moved across the river first, then the animals. On the bank were about 1,000 natives who had crossed over to Rosario after Bubb's detachment began its march. They were friendly, especially at Hacienda de Dominicos—which was a relief. The march was uneventful through Santa Cruz to the iron bridge connecting with the Hacienda de Agustinos, where the flanking column camped.

After detailing a company of infantry to guard the expedition's base at Rosario, the principal column moved out about 2:30 P.M. for San Francisco de Malabon. The column was organized in the usual manner with Captain Reilly leading and the center platoon under First Sergeant Follinsby in the advance ·guard. When they were about a mile from Rosario enemy troops were observed about 2 miles away, apparently preparing to deploy west of San Francisco. They were quickly dispersed by the shrapnel fire of the leading piece of Follinsby's platoon. That night the command was strung out in bivouac in the road from a point opposite the iron bridge back to the Hacienda de Agustinos, a conglomeration of massive buildings dating back to the 18th century and enclosed by a high, loopholed stone wall. The wagon train and rear guard were encamped within the enclosed area. Some of the wagons did not arrive until early the next morning, their road being the worst encountered thus far. The road to the south was equally bad, so to save time in the morning, a passageway wide enough for the artillery was cut through the thicket that night on each side of the road. A small reconnoitering party under Lieutenants Castner and Fuller made its way to the enemy's outposts near the edge of San Francisco where they captured a native who, although apparently intelligent, refused to divulge any information.

Orders were given in the evening for a simultaneous forward movement of the columns on the opposite sides of the Cañas. The teams hitched to the wagons were to remain at the hacienda, guarded by a detachment from the cavalry troop; the balance of the troop was stationed at the iron bridge to maintain contact between the two columns or to assist either. Major Bubb was instructed to act according to circumstances. If he found no enemy in his front, he was to cross to the right bank of the river and attack San Francisco from the west; or, failing to effect a crossing there, he could if necessary return to the bridge and support the left column. In the event of the enemy's flight or retreat, he was to pursue his march up the river, keeping abreast of and in touch with the column on the other side as far as practicable.

The troops moved forward at daybreak on October 10 as planned. The advance guard of the left or principal column consisted of Lieutenant H. T. Fergueson's battalion of the Thirteenth Infantry (Companies A, H, and M), which was preceded at some distance by Castner's scouts and by one piece of artillery under the immediate direction of Captain Reilly. After proceeding cautiously about half a mile, the gun, commanded by Sergeant Follinsby, opened fire and cleared the roads at those points where the previous evening's reconnaissance had discovered the enemy's intrenchments. Lieutenant Fergueson, after deploying one company to the left of the road, which drove a party of insurgents from a trench, advanced steadily with the entire battalion until it reached the town. He then encircled the town with outposts that commanded all exit roads. The main body soon arrived and was held for a time in the streets, pending an examination of the town from which all the inhabitants had fled precipitately that morning. The enemy had been in San Francisco and Santa Cruz in considerable force the day before but had apparently decided that it was useless to fight the American troops as a body and had resorted to a stratagem that was expected to baffle the Americans. General Trias, who was believed to be in command, had practically disbanded the mass of his soldiers, many of whom lived in the area, but he retained 6 or 7 companies that were to be used to harass the Americans in every way possible.

There were indications that these organizations had retreated intact toward Buena Vista. Accordingly, 4 companies of Captain Woodbridge Geary's battalion, the Thirteenth Infantry (Companies C, G, K, and L), with one gun accompanied by Captain Reilly and detachments of the signal and hospital corps, were sent out on the Buena Vista road at 9:30 A.M. This road, running southerly, was closely hedged in by bamboo and flanked at distances ranging from 50 to 500 yards by the Cañas on the west and by a deep stream with high banks on the east. This afforded the enemy excellent opportunities for firing into the column on the road with comparatively little danger to himself.

Soon after clearing San Francisco, Captain Geary's advance guard (Company K) engaged the enemy lying in ambush, driving him slowly but steadily to the south and southeast. The fighting was continuous along this road for about half a mile. The sound of the firing from Bubb's column west of the Cañas indicated that he, too, was pushing the enemy south. In this advance the flankers of Captain Geary's advance guard captured, some distance east of the road, a rebel hospital flying the Red Cross flag where they found 2 dead and 5 wounded insurgents and a storehouse. The contents of the latter consisted of large quantities of clothing, khaki cloth, and other military supplies, and an estimated 8,000 rounds of Mauser and Remington ammunition—all of which were destroyed under orders from brigade headquarters. When the column subsequently returned to San Francisco it was reported by Lieutenant P. E. Pierce that 5 dead and 24 wounded insurgents were found in the hospital. To quote from Lieutenant Pierce's report: "Evidently the attendants had gone into the fields and gathered up their injured after we had pushed on."

At a point little more than a mile from San Francisco, General Schwan joined Captain Geary's advance troop. At this time the enemy, about 300 strong, appeared to be slowly retreating southward on the road parallel to the river on the left, and also in a southeasterly direction across the rice fields. The pursuit was vigorously continued for about 600 yards when a short halt was ordered. Company L was placed in the lead when the advance was resumed, relieving Lieutenant Pierce's Company K. This was the company that had taken the hospital and warehouse and had also captured a number of prisoners, including a lieutenant colonel and one other officer. Shortly afterward the enemy suddenly opened fire from their intrenchments in the immediate front on the infantry skirmishers. Captain Geary, who was with the support of the advance guard, was killed.

Both Companies K and L were immediately moved up, Company G was ordered to cover the left flank, and Company C remained in reserve on the road. A fierce fight ensued in the course of which "Reilly's piece was run to the front by hand and did splendid execution." The enemy was soon driven off and, splitting up into small groups that fled to the southeast, disappeared from the front. The bridge commander subsequently ordered a company under Lieutenant F. W. Coleman Jr., Thirteenth Infantry, in pursuit. It crossed the river on the left, proceeded over rice fields for about 1½ miles, and returned about 3 P.M. without having encountered the enemy.

About this time, Major Bubb, who had been moving up the left bank of the Cañas, ordered Lieutenant E. B. Gose with Company D, Thirteenth Infantry, to communicate with the principal column on the other side of the Cañas and to report to the brigade commander for instructions. Bubb's column had moved forward at daybreak according to plan. Steady but slight resistance was encountered. At a point about 2 miles from the bridge, however, the insurgents seemed to be determined to make a firm stand. Lieutenant McCloskey's platoon had been marching along the road, which was skirted on the right side with nipa huts and banana and mango trees for a width of 50 yards, and beyond this was a great expanse of rice fields. On the left side of the road were huts and dense growths extending to the river bank. The infantry, deployed as skirmishers, advanced through the rice fields toward the position occupied by the insurgents. The two guns, concealed by the heavy growth, marched close to the rice fields away from the road and in the same line as the skirmishers.

At about 800 yards from a ridge occupied by the enemy, a favorable opening in the undergrowth gave the guns a clear field of fire in front of the infantry toward the enemy. Here the two guns were brought into action, the animals being led down into the sunken road. After a short action of 20 or 30 minutes, the enemy's fire was silenced. The column then advanced another mile and halted for noon. During this halt Lieutenants McCloskey and Stickle, the engineer officer of the flanking column, reconnoitered the ridge that had been held by the enemy. At one point, evidently an outpost, a dead Filipino was found with his shoulder torn off and his chest ripped open by a shapnel fragment. By his side were a Remington rifle and cartridge belt that were taken and turned in. Major Bubb, not finding either the bridge shown on the maps or any other practicable crossing, continued to advance about 2½ miles south and west of San Francisco. From there, complying with instructions received through Lieutenant Gose and having completed his assigned mission, he returned to the iron bridge and encamped at the same place as on the previous night.

There being no sign of the enemy, Captain Geary's battalion, now taken over by Lieutenant Pierce, also returned to San Francisco de Malabon, joining the main body of the principal column in its bivouac there.

Before going out on the Buena Vista road General Schwan had telegraphed the division commander, Major General H. W. Lawton, that to avoid destruction the enemy had dissipated his forces. He suggested that the question of garrisoning these important towns, comprising a population of about 24,000, be considered as a means of counteracting the effect of this dispersion and to determine the status of each individual in the community as either friend or foe. This proposal was turned down by the department commander owing to the lack of troops at his disposal.

The brigade commander made a reconnaissance in the direction of Dasmariñas, and on his return he reported to the division commander that the road was impassable for cavalry or wheeled vehicles and was suitable only for foot troops. On the following day, October 11, the dismounted troops, carrying three days' rations individually, were prepared to start for the Imus road. The mounted troops and wagon train were to retrace their march to Bacoor. The separation of the command into two parts and the requisite preparations for the march occupied the entire day. Fifty-two flintlock guns and a small brass cannon, discovered in a hiding place at San Francisco de Malabon, and files of personnel rolls, returns, and records belonging to General Trias (except a few saved for future reference) were destroyed. Two reconnaissances, one by Lieutenant Stickle during which fire was exchanged with the enemy, and the other, led by Captain Wm. L. Sibers and Lieutenants Castner and Hawkins, were made to determine the best trail across the rice fields to the Imus road. In consonance with the corps commander's policy not to hold any persons except insurgents in confinement unless their release might jeopardize the safety of the troops, about two hundred prisoners who had been captured at various places were released early the following morning. Some sixty of them were employed and rendered excellent service carrying supplies across the rice fields. They were paid the same compensation that the Chinese coolies attached to the troops received for similar services. The release of the prisoners also eliminated a heavy guard burden that would otherwise have hampered the mobile column.

During the morning of the 11th Major Bubb's detachment moved out of its camp near the iron bridge. Lieutenant McCloskey's platoon, with a detachment of infantry as escort, marched to the mouth of the Cañas, crossed it, and camped at Rosario. Captain Reilly and the other platoon arrived there that afternoon with two Filipino officer prisoners. The cavalry troop, the wagon train, and ambulances were also assembled at Rosario. The sick and wounded and all surplus supplies were transferred to Lieutenant Cunningham's launch and taken to Manila. Major Bubb's battalion and the company of infantry that had been left at Rosario joined their several organizations at San Francisco. On the following day, the 12th, Captain Reilly marched both platoons back to Imus with the wagon train, returning through Noveleta, Cavite Viejo, and Binacayan. The next day the two platoons marched from Imus to Bacoor, preceding the main body of the column.

It was noted previously that San Francisco was practically deserted when the troops went in to occupy it, but before their departure a considerable number of inhabitants returned to their homes, bringing back with them the belongings they had concealed in the woods. They had probably been encouraged to return by their "padre," in whom they seemed to have implicit confidence. This man, while disclaiming sympathy with the insurrection and professing loyalty to the American cause, maintained close relations with the rebel leaders and kept a large amount of rice and other supplies in a building connected with his luxuriously furnished house. His true sentiments were an enigma. General Schwan finally concluded it was best not to interfere with either his money (he had $2,000 in Mexican silver) or the stock of provisions he had accumulated on the padre's solemn protestation that the poor people in the town would starve if the supplies were destroyed or confiscated.

Daybreak of October 12 found the command in readiness to start for Dasmariñas without any wheeled vehicles and divested of all impedimenta. That portion of its line of march from San Francisco to the barrio of Malagasan (Primo), a distance of 4½ miles that passed through one continuous rice field intersected by two rivers and many small and two large irrigation ditches, merits a brief description. As in other parts of the island, the rice was grown in rectangular plots averaging about 100 by 300 feet. These plots were separated by earthen ridges or dikes about 18 inches high. The irrigation ditches, large and small, were so arranged that any plot or series of plots could be flooded at will. During the growing season the plots were kept flooded to a depth of 2 to 3 inches. Before the rice was set out, the ground was plowed to a depth of 5 to 6 inches. It was during this growing season that the fields had to be crossed.

The terrain was most difficult for the marching troops. Since the rice dikes were narrow and the footing insecure, many soldiers fell or slid into the mud on either side. Inasmuch as the march was made in several single-file columns on parallel dikes, it was prudent to form an advance line sloshing through the water and mud of the rice plots. General Schwan and his staff rode across the fields, partly as an experiment to determine the possibility and practicability of crossing them. A horse often found very soft ground just beyond the dike with his front feet while his hind feet were still on the dike—with the result that sometimes the rider involuntarily crossed the dike ahead of his horse.

It was found that the horses could cross the rice fields while the plots were flooded. The larger irrigation ditches, which generally had a soft bottom, were the most difficult obstacles. The streams also presented serious but not insurmountable obstacles. When the head of the column reached the Ilang Ilang River, Castner's scouts, who were in the lead, bore off to the left, following what they thought was a well-beaten trail. The remainder of the column headed straight for the Imus road and reached it ahead of the scouts.

Two rebel soldiers, captured as the column filed into the Imus road, stated that eight insurgent companies were occupying the towns of Sabang and Dasmariñas, three companies at the former and five at the latter; also that other rebel troops were at Silang and Buena Vista. Believing a fight to be imminent, Castner sent a courier to Imus with the request that a gun, if one could be spared, and an ambulance be sent under proper escort to join the command at Dasmariñas. After a brief rest, the troops moved off toward Sabang and Dasmariñas, but no enemy was found in either barrio. That night the command bivouacked in the road.

Before going into bivouac, one reconnoitering party was sent out on the Silang road and another on the road to Buena Vista. The first party proceeded some 2 or 3 miles and fired a few shots at straggling insurgents. After dark the requested ambulance and gun, and also an entire battalion under Captain Cowles, Fourth Infantry, joined the column, coming from Imus. Although the scouting party had failed to locate the enemy in any considerable force within several miles to the south and west, it was thought that the opportunity should not be missed to make a show of force at Buena Vista and Silang. Both towns were known to be the centers of insurgent activity and concentration points of insurgent troops. Orders were therefore given for two battalions to move on Buena Vista at daybreak on October 13, and another column was to march to Silang at a later hour. During the night, however, a message was received from division headquarters conveying the department commander's order that the column return as soon as practicable. Accordingly the column marched to Imus the next morning and proceeded to Bacoor in the evening, where it was disbanded, and the organizations composing it returned to their various stations.

Throughout this expedition one gun was always with the advance party of the vanguard and one was with the support. These two sections, in advance of the main column, had to cut roads through cane fields, tear down fences and obstacles, and then fight with their guns. Their task was hard. General Schwan in his report of the expedition into the province of Cavite, October 7-14, 1899, stated: "The work of the artillery, arduous in the extreme owing to the condition of the roads, may without exaggeration be characterized as brilliant. Under the leadership of their dashing officers [Captain Taylor, Captain Reilly, and Lieutenant McCloskey], one or more sections were invariably placed on the firing line; in one instance [on the Buena Vista road], where the troops were obliged to move forward in column, the leading piece marched with the point of the advance guard." General Schwan's report also stated, "As has already been pointed out, the expedition was hastily organized, and consisted of organizations not one of which had previously served with any other. Nevertheless, all worked well together from the start; officers and men alike seemed eager to accomplish whatever task was given them. In fact the command, good at the start, improved steadily, and when broken up was fit and anxious to undertake any service, however arduous."

For the next several months the center platoon of the battery, First Sergeant Follinsby commanding under the direction of Captain Reilly, was stationed at Bacoor; the right platoon, Lieutenant McCloskey commanding, was at Imus; and the left platoon, Lieutenant Summerall commanding, was at Calamba. It was while the center platoon was at Bacoor that the artillerymen saw their first Filipino funeral, described by Lieutenant McCloskey in a letter home.

"Bacoor was a squalid town. Its big church down near the bay had great holes in it from the shells thrown by the navy in the fight for the town. For a while the church was used as a hospital but there was a period when there were so many sick that tents were erected on the plaza in front of it to care for the overflow of ill and wounded.

"Follinsby's platoon was parked in the street along one side of the church. The wheels of the guns, limbers, and caissons were coated with mud, and the cannoneers themselves looked tired and jaded as they squatted on the ground around their guns, smoking and talking. It was growing late in the day. A cold rain was falling and the afternoon was beginning to darken. Suddenly the artillerymen heard the sound of a band playing a dirge. Out from a cluster of nearby bamboo houses came a mournful little procession. Three boys marched in front, wearing black capes and carrying wooden crosses; behind them came the band of perhaps twelve instruments, the Filipino musicians dressed in white shirts and trousers; and behind the band came four men carrying a red-draped coffin on their shoulders. A man crying like a child walked after the coffin with a friend at his side who put his arm around the mourner and talked to him in low tones. They were followed by a group of women, one of whom would scream and then sob piteously. A number of boys in the rear completed the procession.

" 'There goes a *good* Filipino,' cynically remarked one soldier who stood watching the funeral. He went on to say that the man being buried had been killed fighting near Imus the day before. His relatives had brought the body into town during the night so that it might be decently buried. The man behind the coffin was the dead man's brother, and the crying and screaming woman was his widow. The cortege walked slowly down the road. They did not heed the rain splashing in their faces as they sloshed along in the mud in their bare feet without looking up. The three boys with the wooden crosses straggled along in front. One walked on the sidewalk the soldiers had put down; another stuck sturdily to his place in the middle of the street, and the third walked with the musicians.

"It was a sad and shabby looking little band. Their white clothes were wet and limp, and splashed with mud. One of the players was blind and was being led by a boy. Some of the musicians walked in a little group in front. The blind man and two others followed a few yards behind, while the drummer, an old man who could hardly keep up, stumbled along last. A gust blew off the hat of one of the musicians and carried it scurrying down the muddy road, but the owner gave no sign that he noticed its loss. He walked on bareheaded in the rain, playing as before. The little procession splashed on in the rain and mud toward the cemetery.

"A company of the Fourteenth Infantry, which had been out fighting for three or four days, came swinging back to its camp in Bacoor. The funeral procession huddled over against the wall on one side of the road to let the soldiers pass. The sturdy Americans, with their rifles slung on their shoulders, swung by the small brown men with the battered old horns, standing in the rain around the gaudy red coffin and the three wooden crosses.

"The procession passed on down the road. The band was now playing a wild, barbaric melody that seemed in keeping with the cold, cheerless rain, the heavy black clouds in the sky, the dark, sullen afternoon, the wailing of the winds in the bamboo, and the pitiful procession of barefoot mourners. Soon the funeral party disappeared through the open gates of the cemetery.

"The cannoneers had long since sought the shelter of their tents."

During the next several months the three platoons were continuously engaged with the infantry troops in fighting the Filipino insurgents. A few examples of their operations are illustrative of their employment until the platoons were reunited under Captain Reilly at the Exposition Grounds in Manila on February 8, 1900. The battery historian wrote:

"On November 20, a battalion of the Fourth Infantry commanded by Captain W. H. Cowles made a reconnaissance to Puente Julian, 1¼ miles from Imus. One gun of the [McCloskey's] platoon was posted so as to command the advance of the infantry, having a rice field varying from 100 to 300 yards wide and 2,200 yards long in its front. The other gun under Sergeant Proctor was posted at an outpost on the south face of the town having also a clear field of fire over rice paddies to the crossroad on which the battalion would march. Sergeant Proctor was instructed to keep his front free of the enemy but not to fire at a point on the crossroad nearer than 500 yards from the road leading back to Imus. By intelligent bursting of shrapnel, Sergeant Proctor kept this flank free of the enemy and incidentally inflicted heavy losses on them when they were exposed to the cross fire of the two guns, this one and the other which later joined the battalion.

"When about a mile from the town, the infantry became heavily involved. Owing to the dense bamboo growth bordering the rice fields, it was impossible to tell where the infantry was, and in order to make his fire more effective, the platoon commander had the piece limbered up and galloped to the relief of the battalion. As the section galloped down to the crossroad 2200 yards from its outpost it was subjected to a heavy fire. At the crossroad, the piece was brought into action and fired 5 or 6 shots over the scouts about 300 yards in advance. Deeming this unsafe, the platoon commander moved the piece to the line occupied by the scouts, the most advanced line, on the bank of a stream whose far side was held by the enemy. As the piece was unlimbered here, the wheel horse 'Grant' was killed. The piece was run by hand to the bank and there did good work, its very proximity to the enemy demoralizing them. Private Wetherby, Fourth Infantry, delivered a message from Captain Cowles to Lieutenant McCloskey to cease firing and return to Imus, and on his return from this errand [the orderly] was mortally wounded, afterwards receiving a medal of honor."

Lieutenant McCloskey, by constant repetition, had drummed into his artillerymen, "Never touch a wound with your hand or fingers —lest you transmit infection." And it was during the fighting just related that a Mauser rifle bullet went through the brim of the hat worn by Private Lievre. Being fully indoctrinated, he ran to his commander to report loudly, "I kept my hand off the wound."

During this same engagement Lieutenant McCloskey's horse "Pet" was shot twice, once through the flesh at the forearm and again through the hind leg close to the bow midway between hock and fetlock. As a result of careful treatment his only permanent injury was a small bone growth that was not obvious at a casual glance, and within three weeks he had recovered and returned to duty. He did service later in China and again in the Philippines. In 1906, more than six years later, McCloskey, now a captain, was transferred from Fort Ethan Allen, Vermont, to Jolo in the Sulu Sea. En route he stopped in Manila and visited the field artillery camp there. The battery commander and the stable sergeant assured him that they had only one horse from Reilly's battery, and he was named "Peking." Captain McCloskey had a hunch and asked to see the horse. He ran his hand gently down the horse's leg till he found the small growth and asked the captain, "Feel this." Then he asked the sergeant if the horse could perform any tricks. "No, sir, he is just a horse." This was too much for McCloskey. He grasped the halter strap, patted his neck, and put his cheek on the horse's upper lip. Then he put his hand down and said "Up, Pet," and old Pet raised his foot and planted it squarely in Father's hand! The captain and sergeant agreed, "He's your horse, all right." Pet had not forgotten also that he was usually rewarded with sugar for his act, and fortunately Father had a lump or two in his pocket as he always did when he visited a stable.

The historian's account continues:

"On November 25 about 2:30 A.M. the command at Imus was alarmed by a vicious and heavy fire on the outposts. Both guns of the platoon had been left at the outposts and were soon in action. The night was moonlit, and a constant fire was kept up until broad daylight. At the outposts where the guns were stationed the platoon commander had previously determined the range to prominent objects by means of the rangefinder and later by trial shots. In case of night attacks the gunner had only to direct his piece toward any prominent point and give it the proper elevation. By changing the direction of the piece and the elevation, a large field of fire was covered. The insurgents were advancing through the rice fields cheering and calling out, 'Americano no good, mucha jawbone.' As dawn came, their fire slackened and they gradually dispersed to their homes. Their number was estimated at 2,000 to 3,000. From reports brought in later, they suffered more than 100 casualties on this night."

On January 6, 1900, Sergeant Follinsby's center platoon, 3rd piece, under direction of Captain Reilly, marched to Binacayan and crossed the Imus River, with the gun being taken across on a cascoe and the horses swimming over. The following day it accompanied a battalion of the Twenty-eighth Infantry, Colonel Birkhimer commanding, to Putol Bridge, engaging the strongly intrenched insurgents on the Noveleta road from 7 to 9 A.M., when they were driven out. Two horses were killed and two artillerymen wounded, one of whom, Musician Protz, was shot through the left shoulder. A few days later the center platoon marched with a battalion of the Fourth Infantry, under Major Scott, to Putol Bridge. It was joined there by Troop A, Eleventh Cavalry, then it proceeded to Noveleta where it camped for the night. The next day it continued the march by way of Rosario to San Francisco de Malabon where it remained encamped until the end of the month, although it accompanied reconnaissance parties daily.

On January 1, 1900, the left platoon under Lieutenant Summerall, with one 3.2-inch gun, one Hotchkiss, and one Gatling gun, left Calamba at 4 A.M. with a battalion of the Thirty-ninth Infantry, driving the enemy from his trenches and through Cabongas and Santa Rosa. After camping at Santa Rosa it renewed the advance early the next morning, fighting continuously and driving the insurgents through San Pedro de Tomas and Carmona, and camping at

9. Officers in the Philippines, 1899. Left to right: Lieutenant Bowley, Lieutenant Kilbreth, Captain Taylor, Captain Reilly, Lieutenant Miller, Lieutenant Summerall, Lieutenant McCloskey.

Biñan. On January 9 Lieutenant Summerall left Calamba at 4 A.M. with his platoon and the same three guns to accompany again a battalion of the Thirty-ninth Infantry. The enemy was driven from his trenches on Santo Tomas road and from several successive lines. After capturing the Puente de Viga it reached Santo Tomas at 2 P.M. on the 10th and started back to Calamba; but while on the march it received orders to reoccupy Santo Tomas. The river crossings were prepared, and on the following morning the enemy's position on the hill back of Santo Tomas was attacked by Cheatham's battalion of the Thirty-seventh Infantry and taken. The American units left the hill at 6 A.M. on the 13th, joining the Thirty-ninth Infantry at Tanauan and overtaking the Thirty-eighth Infantry at 9 A.M., when Lieutenant Summerall's platoon joined the advance guard. Contact was established at 10 A.M. with the insurgents, who were in an intrenched position but were driven out after an hour's fighting. The American troops entered Lipa that afternoon and continued their pursuit of the enemy through Rosario, Ibaan, and Batangas in the province of Batangas, and back to Santa Cruz in Laguna province. This was the pattern of the operations of Lieutenant Summerall's platoon until it rejoined the other platoons of Captain Reilly's battery in Manila.

On February 2, 1900, the center platoon, Sergeant Follinsby commanding under the direction of Captain Reilly, left San Francisco de Malabon and marched to Imus where it camped adjacent to Lieutenant McCloskey's platoon. The following morning the two platoons marched to Manila and went into quarters at the Exposition Grounds. Lieutenant Summerall's left platoon, with one gun, returned to Calamba from Santa Cruz on February 5. Three days later the platoon left Calamba on cascoes and arrived at Manila on February 9 to join the rest of the battery on the Exposition Grounds.

On March 14 Captain Reilly's battery marched to Guadaloupe Heights to conduct experimental firing tests with shells containing a bursting charge of a new explosive, "thorite." During April, May, and June the battery also engaged in experimental firing of one Hotchkiss and one Maxim-Nordenfeldt mountain gun for the Ordnance Department, U.S. Army, to determine questions relating to ammunition and recoil. These projects ended abruptly early in July when the battery received orders to prepare to go to China for duty in the ugly situation there.

Chapter III

Rise of the Boxers

Anyone who is familiar with the various Chinatowns of our Western world knows the tremendous influence their secret societies have over their members. In the 1890's political and economic conditions contributed greatly to the growth of the Boxers in China. The Boxers were a secret society that inherited their title from an ancient religious brotherhood. For years China had been honeycombed with societies of all kinds for all purposes; even thieves and beggars were thoroughly organized. The I Ho Ch'uan Society, or Fist of the Patriotic Union, generally translated as "Big Sword," "Big Knife," or "Boxers," had been in existence for many years but became known under the latter name in the late 1890's.

Membership in the Boxer movement grew rapidly in a period of wide discontent. In the fall of 1898 disastrous floods covered about 2,500 miles of Shantung territory, which had a population of between 1,000,000 and 1,500,000. By the end of the year Northern Kiangsu Province had had two bad crop years, resulting in famine, unrest, and large-scale banditry. These conditions soon spread an Anhwei and Shantung. By the following spring the situation was so bad in Northern Kiangsu that children were sold for 50 to 1,000 copper cash each. After missionaries were involved in disturbances in Shantung, the movement of discontent was concentrated against foreigners.

China was full of dissatisfaction caused by the growth and influence of Western powers. It began with the Opium War (1839-42) with Great Britain, which resulted in China's being forced to grant commercial concessions and to recognize the principle of exterritoriality, the privilege of exemption from local law and law enforcement while in a foreign country. The concessions to Great Britain were soon followed by others to France, Germany, and Russia. The Manchu (Ch'ing) Dynasty, weakened by these European encroachments, was further debilitated by Japan's success in the First Sino-Japanese War (1894-95) that further partitioned China into foreign spheres of influence. The construction of the Trans-Siberian Railway, begun in 1891, quickened after Russia and China bound themselves by the Li-Lobanov Alliance of 1896 to mutual support in opposition to any aggression by Japan against Russian East Asia, China, or Korea. The U.S. annexation of the Philippine Islands in 1898 after the war with Spain projected our interests in the Far East.

Kuang Hsu, the Ch'ing emperor, attempted to meet the threat of modernization by adopting modern ways and customs himself, but Chinese resentment had grown too strong. His attempt at compromise was frustrated in 1898 by the Dowager Empress Tz'u Hsi, who favored a last effort to expel foreign influence by supporting armed resistance. Tz'u Hsi, born Yehonala, became the Imperial Concubine of Emperor Hsieh Feng, and after his death in 1861 her baby son became Emperor T'ung Chih. She and the Empress Consort became Empress Dowagers through an edict issued in the name of the infant ruler. With the help of Hsien Feng's brother, Prince Kung, they overthrew the established regency and won the palladium of authority.

Tz'u Hsi, who possessed the typical strengths and weaknesses of the period, began to gather the reins of authority into her hands. The Emperor T'ung Chih died in 1875, reportedly of smallpox, but it was rumored that the true cause was the wild excesses urged by Tz'u Hsi. She promptly broke the established rules of succession by prevailing on the court to have her infant son selected for the throne. Anticipating her probable fate, T'ung Chih's widowed consort committed suicide. Six years later Tz'u An, the other Empress Dowager, died. Poison was suspected but never investigated. Finally in 1884 Tz'u Hsi relieved Prince Kung, an experienced statesman, of all his duties. It appears that she had harbored a long-time dislike for Prince Kung because of his role in the execution of a favored eunuch.

Tz'u Hsi had now consolidated her control of authority. Until 1884 Prince Kung had provided wise counsel in the conduct of China's foreign affairs, but his advice and guidance were completely obliterated by Tz'u Hsi's bigotry in the administration of China's affairs of state. A new favorite eunuch, Li Lien-ying, encouraged Tz'u Hsi's vices and promoted her unwise rule of the nation. In 1889 she gave up her regency and retired to the Summer Palace on the outskirts of Peking, and her nephew, Emperor Kuang Hsu, who had married her elder niece—selected by Tz'u Hsi—and was of age, was to ascend the throne.

Kuang Hsu was expected to follow the general administrative policies previously established by Tz'u Hsi, and although she admitted that some updating of the policies was required, she anticipated that these changes would be modest reforms of a self-strengthening nature recommended by Chinese moderates during the 1880-90 era. But after the war with Japan, Kuang Hsu was deeply concerned with the growing division within China. As a boy and later as a young man he had learned English and read many books on Western subjects. As a result he was well informed on the conflict of ideas between the Western and Chinese viewpoints. In earlier years Tz'u Hsi had approved the sending of selected bright young Chinese abroad for courses of study. Many of these men became outstanding statesmen, and they along with Kuang Hsu were undoubtedly influenced by their studies.

Following the Sino-Japanese War many educated Chinese became convinced that their country would never again become strong until certain reforms were effected in the government and the corruption terminated. A society was formed by T'an Ssu-t'ung to promote Western learning, which emerged as a sort of political organization with the aim of bringing about essential reforms. The idea was widely accepted, and soon other clubs with the same goals were formed. About the same time another Chinese patriot, K'ang Yu-wei, wrote a document ("Ten Thousand Word Memorial") protesting the terms of the Treaty of Saimonoseki (April 1895), which gave Japan the Liaotung Peninsula, Formosa, and the Pescadores, and he obtained the signatures of some twelve thousand officials in eighteen provinces on the document. He organized a club called the Society of National Rejuvenation, which established offices in Peking and Shanghai.

As the movement gained momentum and publicity it came to the attention of Weng T'ung-ho, the Emperor's tutor, who also held the post of Grand Secretary. Weng's sympathies were with the reformists, and it was he who brought K'ang's Memorial to the Emperor's attention. K'ang also sent books relating to the reforms in Japan and Russia for Kuang Hsu to read. Thus the Emperor became identified with the reformists. With the loyal Pearl Concubine (favorite concubine of an emperor) at his side, the now adult Emperor defied his Imperial father and Tz'u Hsi. The court was divided into two factions. Tz'u Hsi and the Manchus of high standing—who would lose everything if the reforms were effected—were on one side. The Emperor had Weng and a number of other free-thinking reformists on his side. The Emperor's faction was strengthened when Weng introduced K'ang to Kuang Hsu. The Emperor liked K'ang so well that Weng arranged for him to be appointed as Assistant Grand Secretary at the Ministry of Foreign Affairs (Tsungli Yamen).

June 11, 1898, marked the beginning of the Hundred Days Reform period. It began with the appointment of K'ang as chief of the newly created Office of Constitution, which indicated that the Emperor planned to give the nation a constitution. Tz'u Hsi and her followers were alarmed and struck quickly. Weng was removed from his post and exiled in the country. Tz'u Hsi also named the unscrupulous Jung Lu Viceroy of Chihli and Commissioner for North China and put him on the Grand Council.

Despite this setback the Emperor had the strength of will to resolve to initiate the reform program. The revising of the educational system of China was instituted. Decree after decree was rapidly issued to eliminate the worn-out system of essays and sonnets in civil service examinations, and the sciences and practical arts of the modern world were substituted. To prepare for the new tests a system of common schools was planned, using Buddhist, Taoist, and Confucian temples. Middle schools were to be set up in all districts and colleges established in the provinces. A new university was to be founded in Peking for the graduates of provincial institutions and the sons of the nobility. The reforms were not restricted to education. Sinecures in the Mandarinate were abolished. New bureaus for agriculture, commerce, and mining were created. It was also suggested that the Emperor's male subjects cut off their queues.

One of the most important actions was to grant his people the right of free speech, ordaining that even junior officers should have the right to address the Throne without hindrance or obstruction. This was the blow that shattered the reform program. A young doctor in the Han Lin Academy of literary dignitaries proposed a number of administration changes in the government. His chiefs, all of whom were old men, refused to forward the document to the Throne. When the Emperor learned that they had prevented one of his officials from conferring with him, he stripped them of their official honors and threatened to dismiss them from the public service.

Smarting under their punishment, the chiefs hurried to the Country Palace and, throwing themselves at the feet of the Empress Dowager, implored her to come out of retirement and save the nation from the young Emperor. Tz'u Hsi, who had twice before been Regent, had never completely retired from politics, and even before the visit of the old chiefs she had prepared for such an emergency. An army of picked troops was moved to Tientsin under Jung Lu; another army was stationed near Peking. This action was followed by an announcement that Tz'u Hsi and the Emperor would make an inspection at Tientsin in the near future. Realizing that some plot was being hatched, the Emperor and his advisers decided to move quickly.

Knowing that Weng had always held Yuan Shih-k'ai, commander of the army in Shantung, in high esteem, and learning that Yuan favored the cause of the reformists, they summoned him to Peking and appointed him Vice-President of the War Board. A short time later Yuan was surprised to receive a visit from T'an, who was a trusted adviser to the Emperor, at his living quarters in Peking. As nearly as can be determined, T'an convinced Yuan that Jung Lu was involved in a plot to overthrow and murder the Emperor; and he reportedly showed Yuan a secret order from the Emperor directing Yuan to proceed to Tientsin, execute Jung Lu, take over his command and all rail and telegraph services, bring his army to Peking to guard the Forbidden City (the innermost citadel inside the walls of Peking), and lay siege to the Summer Palace of the Empress Dowager.

As soon as T'an departed, Yuan went immediately to Tientsin and related the whole story to Jung Lu—who hurried to Peking to inform the Empress. Within forty-eight hours, Tz'u Hsi left the Summer Palace and returned to the Forbidden City, where she announced her regency. Kuang Hsu was separated from his Pearl Concubine and imprisoned in one of the palaces. K'ang escaped and lived in Europe and America for many years. Several of the Reformists, including T'an, were captured and executed. For his services Yuan acquired great wealth and later became the Provisional President of China (February 15, 1912). The only institution established by the young Emperor that Tz'u Hsi permitted to continue was the new university founded by Li Hung Chang, one of the leading proponents of educational reforms in the Chinese Empire.

Shortly before the Empress became Regent for the third time, Germany had seized the seaport of Kiaochow in reprisal for the killing of two of her missionaries in the southern part of Shantung. Russia immediately demanded Port Arthur, and thereupon England insisted on having Wei Hai Wei, on the opposite shore, in order to keep track of Russia's operations. In the far south, France protested being left out and demanded that the political balance should be preserved by giving her the Bay of Kwangchowan, near her Annamite Empire borders. Being unprepared to wage war, the Empress was forced to make these cessions, but she made it known to her people that, unprepared or not, she would declare war if any other nation pressed for similar cessions.

The resentment felt by the members of the reform group over the Sino-Japanese debacle and the growth and interference of Western power was also shared by the Boxers. Some important differences existed, however, between the two factions. The reformists were scholarly, educated individuals, whereas the Boxers in the early stages were peasants. K'ang appealed to their reason, but he was prepared to use force if need be to achieve his goal. With their limited education the Boxers envisaged only one way to accomplish their objective—freedom from the foreigners—and that was by bloodshed. Although the Boxers were a patriotic society, there is some question as to which dynasty they supported. But they had never forgotten that their masters were foreigners. Their motto was inscribed on the cards left with the Christians whom they robbed: "Pao Ch'ing Mieh Yang," which translates as "China for the Chinese, Death to Foreigners."

The avowed objective of the Boxers from the beginning was to expel all foreigners from the country. It was a natural outgrowth of antiforeign feeling. When the Chinese saw the Americans and Europeans obtaining valuable concessions and preparing to cut up the country with railroads, they were afraid that the invasion would eventually destroy their sacred customs, and that the white man would rule their country. Foreigners were contemptuously referred to as barbarians, but, having been exposed to European firearms, the Chinese also feared the foreigners. A third element, a sense of injustice, also helped to develop the antiforeign feeling. When the Germans occupied Kiaochow they immediately began to build railroads in various directions across Shantung Province, which they claimed as their sphere of influence. The people of Shantung believed that the German government seized upon the murder of the German missionaries as a means of furthering a prearranged political plan. The local newspapers referred to the operation as "German China," but the inhabitants were more aroused by the railroad construction than by any consideration of an infringement of territorial rights. The thought that their cemeteries would be desecrated by the railroad and the spirits of their ancestors awakened by the chugging of the iron monster was too terrible to contemplate.

Leading the fight of the antiforeign Chinese was the secret society of the Boxers. It had been in existence for more than a century, and in 1803 it was formally forbidden by the Chinese government and lapsed into obscurity until the 1890's. It owed its existence to a doctrine that was not orthodox Buddhism, Confucianism, or Taoism, but a superstition based on hypnotism, mesmerism, or spiritualism. Its members engaged in a sort of exercise that was supposed to enable each member to go into a state of trance at will, and when in that condition, he was supposed to possess supernatural strength and also to become bulletproof. In view of possible hostilities with the foreigners, these mysteries were especially attractive, and the

Boxer society grew rapidly among the inhabitants of Shantung. The Manchu governor recognized the organization as an auxiliary force and equipped it with arms.

In Northern China it was essential for the peasants to have two good crops from the land each year to live. The failure of one crop caused widespread suffering, but the failure of both spring and fall crops generally resulted in famine. Crop failure also produced an increased number of highway robberies. Wealthy travelers usually carried firearms for protection but since the diplomats and merchants rarely traveled in the countryside, it was believed that all foreigners were missionaries because they were the only "barbarians" with whom the peasants came in contact. This was one of the reasons why the engineers who traveled into the country to build the railroads were set upon by the Boxers.

In the beginning the missionaries bore the brunt of the attacks because they had gone into the interior of the country, whereas the traders and merchants remained in the treaty ports and coastal towns. The missionaries were attacked not as religious teachers, but as foreigners; and Chinese Christians were murdered and robbed as those who "followed the foreign devils" and not because they had changed their religion.

During the battle for cessions and the land-grabbing tactics of European powers after 1895, many missionaries had begun to assume for themselves the power held by their governments in China. The Chinese provincial official, sensitive to the power plays exerted by foreign governments on his superiors, reacted according to tradition. Unfortunately, many missionaries used this characteristic to their own advantage.

"Drive out the foreigners. Kill the Christians," the Boxers shouted as they traveled through Shantung recruiting their forces. Soon the movement spread to other provinces. Red was considered a lucky color for China, so the Boxer banners were red. Their costumes included red handkerchiefs, red sashes, and red ribbons on their arms and legs. They swore loyalty to their precepts and to each other in elaborate ceremonies in their temples. True, the Boxers attracted a great many of the hopelessly poor, who joined them for plunder, and who would just as quickly desert the cause when booty could no longer be obtained. Faith in the Boxers was not, however, confined to the poorer classes. Tz'u Hsi had begun to listen to reports of the secret society.

The story was told of their invulnerability to an enemy's weapons. Boxer recruits who had performed the secret rites and been initiated were lined up in front of a veteran Boxer. Holding his blunderbuss, the Boxer poured in the powder, then poked down a piece of cotton wadding. A handful of iron buckshot was dropped down the barrel on top of the wadding. The Boxer would gesticulate wildly with his weapon to distract the audience—thus preventing their seeing the buckshot fall out of the weapon as he did so. When the piece was fired from a range of six feet from the intended victims, it emitted a loud noise and considerable flame, but no harm came to the recruits.

The Boxers frequently put on public demonstrations of their invulnerability as a recruiting measure. Crowds usually attended and were entertained and impressed. Bullets were apparently deflected by a wave of the hand, and sword cuts and pike thrusts did no injury to the intended victim. It was inevitable that accidents would occur when the legerdemain failed. Sometimes the results would prove fatal, in which case it was explained that the unfortunate man had undoubtedly broken a law of the society or had not performed his devotions properly—which seemed entirely reasonable to the superstitious Chinese.

Chapter IV

Forebodings in Peking

The Boxer movement originated in the southwest corner of the province of Shantung, which was under the rule of Hu Hsien, as prefect of the department, and Li Ping Hing, as provinicial governor. As a means of checking the comparatively recent foreign aggressions resulting in the seizure of certain parts of China by the Russians, British, and Germans, an Imperial edict was issued after the coup d'etat in 1898 directing every provincial governor to raise a volunteer militia in his province. In a very strong antiforeign province with a notorious antiforeign governor, encouraged by an even more hostile prefect, it was an easy step to incorporate an antiforeign society into the volunteer militia. Being already organized, the Boxer secret society dominated this imperfectly structured militia, and as a result it received official sanction for its existence through the militia. Thus almost from the volunteer outfit's very incipiency it might be said that the Boxers received a kind of encouragement from the government.

Because of the strong antiforeign feeling in the Shantung province —due in part to the introduction of numerous foreign inventions that threw many Chinese out of work, and partly to the seizure of Kiaochow by the Germans, but principally to a strong objection to having their religion and mode of worship changed by the foreign missionaries—there seemed but little doubt that the Boxers, under their early leader, Hu Hsien, were bent on striking a blow against foreign aggression from the outset. The first step taken was against the Chinese Christian converts, or "secondary devils," whom they particularly hated for accepting so despicable a religion; next against the missionaries who were the cause of their religious troubles; next against modern improvements, particularly railroads, which monopolized all transport trade; then against those Chinese who had dealings with foreigners; and finally against the foreign ministers in Peking.

The Germans' demand for the removal of Li Ping Hing was acceded to, but Hu Hsien was appointed governor in his place, and the Boxer movement spread over the province even more rapidly than before. The numerous outrages committed caused the attention of the foreign ministers at Peking to be drawn to the rapid growth and wide extent of the movement and, in accordance with treaty rights, they demanded Hu Hsien's removal. After his forced and reluctant dismissal, he went from Shantung to Peking where, through a friend who was a tutor to the Emperor, he became the adviser of the Dowager Queen. Certainly he never lost her favor, for he was afterward appointed governor of Shansi, the province in which the Imperial household sought refuge when Peking was taken by the foreign forces.

Yuan Shih K'ai, an able official, was then appointed governor of Shantung, and he vigorously set about suppressing the Boxer movement. In fact, he practically routed them out of the province. He decided to conduct a test of their highly touted invulnerability. Lining up a number of them against a wall, he ordered his men to fire. All the Boxers were killed, but even this demonstration failed to shake the public's faith in their supernatural powers.

The province of Chihli, in which Peking is situated, became the hotbed of the Boxers. The whole region between Peking and Paotingfu was alive with them, and Peking itself was threatened. Li Ping Hing, the deposed governor, had settled in Chihli, and the city was considered the seat of the hated foreign devils and their invidious inventions. Many Manchus approved the Boxer activities of attacking mission settlements, burning churches, and killing Christian converts. The Manchus had begun to talk about how the movement could be the salvation of their clan. One of their number, Jung Lu, commissioner for North China, was worried about the developments and the Boxer pretensions to invulnerability. He knew that in one incident in Chihli a Buddhist abbot led his Boxer mob in burning a Christian church and converts' homes. Soldiers fired on the Boxers, killing thirty or forty and capturing their leaders, and again their invulnerability was demonstrated to be a myth to the watching populace. But Jung Lu realized he had not shaken their convictions of supernatural Boxer immunity.

In January 1900, after the murder of an English missionary—a Mr. Brooks, in Shantung Province—all the ministers addressed letters to the Chinese government, calling attention to the extreme gravity of the situation and urging that steps be taken to suppress the society. New incidents from time to time prompted additional letters

Forebodings in Peking

from the ministers. The replies, separate, identical, and joint notes from the Tsungli Yamen, were usually tardy, vague, and generally evasive and unsatisfactory. The ministers were told that the Boxers practiced an innocent kind of gymnastics and if they did sometimes show themselves turbulent and disposed to quarrel with native Christians, it was not without cause. The Empress Dowager also informed the ministers that she intended shortly to issue a decree dismissing the Boxers to their homes. Such decrees were issued but were accompanied by secret instructions to disregard them. In March U.S. Minister Edwin H. Conger suggested the sending of a warship into Chinese waters, but even at that time it was believed in the United States that it was desired more for psychological effect than needed for active service. (Appendix I contains the Proclamation by the Viceroy of Chihli.)

Boxer outrages increased in number and occurred at many different points. Warnings and remonstrances addressed to the Chinese government by the several ministers failed to make the government exert itself to suppress them. The situation was dangerous and threatening, and in the middle of May the ministers called on their respective governments for guards to protect the legations. The Tsungli Yamen was notified that these guards had been summoned and would be arriving immediately.

The guards for the American legation, consisting of a detachment of 48 Marines, 3 blue jackets, and 2 machinists, landed at Taku from the U.S.S. *Oregon* and the *Newark,* commanded by Rear Admiral Louis M. Kempff. They left Tongku by boat on the morning of May 29, arriving in Tientsin about 11 P.M. Permission to travel over the railroad as an armed party had been refused by the viceroy, who would not approve it without the authority of the Tsungli Yamen. Since they were the first foreign troops to arrive in Tientsin, they were received with great enthusiasm by the foreign residents. The detachment remained in Tientsin until Thursday, May 31, waiting for the other legation guards and for permission to go on to Peking.

At 4:30 that afternoon the guards all left by train and reached the railroad station at Machia Fu, outside Peking, about 11 P.M. From there they marched to the city, with the American detachment heading the column, through four miles of silent, densely packed throngs of natives. The American guards were quartered adjoining the legation compound in rear of the Russian bank. At this time, in and around Peking, associating with and friendly to the Boxers, were about 15,000 Imperial Chinese troops under command of Gen-

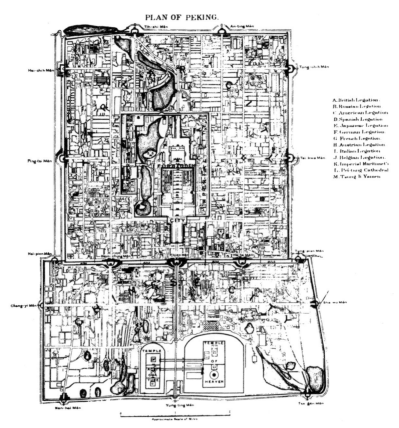

10. Plan of Peking.

eral Tung Fu Hsiang, who was notorious for his hatred of foreigners. No opposition whatever was offered to the entrance of the guards, but steps were soon taken to prevent the arrival of any more. The guards, numbering 350 men, were for the legations of Russia, France, Great Britain, Italy, Japan, and the United States. Their arrival was most reassuring to the foreigners and had the effect of improving the situation in the city, although in the surrounding countryside the Boxers were still active. The German and Austrian guards arrived two days later, and two days after that all railroad and telegraph lines were completely destroyed. Had the ministers waited for the consent of the Chinese government before ordering up the guards, and had their arrival been delayed forty-eight hours, it is unlikely that any foreigner in Peking would have lived to tell the tale of the siege.

The situation outside Peking was growing rapidly worse so that by June 9 the ministers were convinced that the legations' staffs and buildings were in serious danger. (Minister Conger's communications of June 3 and 4, 1900, are contained in Appendix II.) Accordingly they sent messages to the fleet at Taku asking for additional guards who were to come as far as possible by rail and then march overland to Peking. Although they started promptly, the relief party was unable to get through. The call for help had been delayed too long.

Events now followed in quick sequence. On June 12, a fortnight after the arrival of the guards, the chancellor of the Japanese legation was killed at the Yung Ting gate by Boxers and Chinese soldiers of Tung Fu Hsiang. The next day hordes of Boxers entered by the Ha Ta Men (gate) and swept through the city, burning missions and killing and torturing native Christians. For the next several days the Boxers were especially active and set fire not only to churches and mission houses, but also burned down all the native storehouses they suspected of containing foreign goods. Square miles of the city were left strewn with the ruins of the richest business houses in Peking.

The missionaries in the vicinity of Peking gathered at their missions; but all the missions except the Peitang (French), Methodist, and Roman Catholic, were burned on June 13. The Roman Catholic mission and the buildings at the west end of Legation Street were burned on the 14th; and the Chinese City, that part of Peking south of the Tartar Wall, was burned on the 16th, the fire originating in a store which sold foreign goods. The Methodist mission, being the nearest to the legation, was the refuge of the missionaries until they were compelled to enter the compound of the British legation on the 20th.

On June 19 the ministers were informed by the Chinese Foreign Office that the threat to bombard the Taku forts was regarded as an act of war, and that they must leave Peking within twenty-four hours. As a matter of fact, the bombardment had already taken place, and the forts had been captured. The ministers met at once and addressed a note to the Tsungli Yamen protesting that the time was too short to prepare for such a move, inquiring what measures would be taken to insure their safety en route, specifying the least amount of land and water transportation that would be required, and insisting that they be accompanied by some members of the Tsungli Yamen.

For the purpose of reaching an understanding on these questions, they demanded an audience with Princes Ching and Tuan on the following morning and an immediate answer to their note. It was rather fortunate that the ministers found affairs in the city too disturbed for them to visit the Yamen in a body on the next morning as they intended. Baron von Ketteler, the German minister, who went outside the legation against the advice of his colleagues, was killed, and his secretary, Herr Cordes, was wounded on the way. It is more than probable that a similar fate would have befallen the others had they started off. On the same morning a note was received from the Yamen withdrawing the ultimatum of the day before and stating that as the country between Peking and Tientsin was overrun with brigands, it would not be safe for the ministers to go there, and they should therefore remain in Peking.

It had been decided by the foreigners to hold all the legations as long as possible in case of attack, falling back when necessary for united defense on the British legation, where a final stand would be made. The legation, having once been the residence of a high Chinese prince, covered six or eight acres of ground on which there were twenty buildings and was surrounded by strong walls, forming a citadel capable of defense. The order to leave Peking and the murder of Baron von Ketteler hastened matters, and before the time limit fixed by the Chinese had expired at 4 P.M., June 20, all the women, children, and foreign representatives had fled precipitately to the British legation. Sir Claude MacDonald, the British minister, not only welcomed his colleagues, but received all their people, whether civilian or missionary. The missionaries were accompanied by their Catholic and Protestant converts to the number of almost 2,000. An asylum for the converts was secured on the grounds of a Mongol prince on the opposite side of the canal from the legation.

It was well that the foreigners had sought refuge in the British

Forebodings in Peking 75

legation when they did. The rescinding of the ultimatum was intended by the Chinese to lull suspicion, and their treachery was shown when precisely at 4 P.M. Chinese soldiers opened fire on the legations from secret stations at various vantage points. One Frenchman was killed, and an Austrian was wounded.

The Siege of Peking had begun in earnest.

Just a few days later at Paotingfu, about 92 miles from Peking, a number of American missionaries and their children were brutally murdered by the Boxers. A statement of their abuse and death was compiled from information obtained from various persons and sources and is believed to be substantially correct, although little direct testimony of eyewitnesses was secured since there were no survivors to speak for the mission side.

The Presbyterian missionaries, Mr. and Mrs. Simcox, and their three children; Dr. and Mrs. Hodge; and Dr. George Y. Taylor lived in several buildings in one compound near the village of Changchiachuang, which lies about one mile north of the north gate of Paotingfu. On June 30, 1900, between 4 and 5 P.M., the compound was surrounded and attacked by Boxers and villagers. The assault was led by a local Boxer of minor rank, Chu Tu Tze, who was known throughout the city as a ruffian and bad character generally. The day before he had been presented with a gilt button by the niehtai (provincial judge), Ting Yung, who four months later was the fantai, or provincial treasurer. This button, which was worn by Chu Tu Tze at the time of the attack, was in the nature of a decoration or badge of distinction and was presented to him by the niehtai as indicating his appreciation of the man's zeal and energy in the Boxer movement. The incident is mentioned to point out the apparent official sanction of the proceedings on that and the following day.

As soon as the compound was attacked, the missionaries and their children all took refuge in the upper story of one building, where they hoped to defend themselves. All other buildings in the compound were set afire and soon destroyed. A brave defense was made by the besieged, in the course of which Chu Tu Tze was killed and ten Boxers wounded. Dr. Taylor addressed the angry crowd from one of the upper windows in a vain attempt to induce it to disperse, and the Boxers, who did not have firearms, could not dislodge or capture their victims. Finally a successful effort was made to set fire to the building. Soon afterwards the two young Simcox boys, Paul and Francis, aged about 5 and 7 rushed from the building into the open air to escape suffocation from the dense clouds of smoke. They were immediately set upon by the crowd and cut down, and their bodies were thrown into the cistern. The other inmates of the house perished in the flames. The Chinese Christians and servants, about twenty in all, also died, but whether they were killed or were burned to death is not known. One Chinese Christian who tried to kill himself by jumping into the cistern was pulled out and taken to the city. During the night he was tortured in an effort to secure evidence against the missionaries that would corroborate their alleged practices of cutting out eyes, hearts, etc., and of kidnapping children. After the torture, he was murdered.

The American missionaries, the Reverend Mr. Pitkin, Miss Morrell, and Miss Gould, lived in the American Board mission compound in the south suburb of Paotingfu. Mr. and Mrs. Bagnell, one child, and Mr. William Cooper, the English missionaries, lived nearby in another compound. About 7 A.M. on July 1, while local excitement was running very high, the American Board mission compound was attacked by Boxers accompanied by a throng of looting villagers. Mr. Pitkin had already heard of the behavior of the Boxers in attacking the mission to the north of the city, and during the night he prepared for the worst, writing a letter of farewell to his wife and friends and burying it with small articles of personal and church property near the corner of the house. These pitiful relics were dug up by the Chinese and never recovered. The two women, who had occupied a house at the farther end of the compound, had moved to Mr. Pitkin's house. Upon being attacked they all took refuge, first in the chapel and later in a smaller building nearby. Mr. Pitkin was armed with a revolver and defended his charges until his ammunition was gone. Thereupon the mob poured into the house, seized the exhausted little group and dragged them out. In the melee Mr. Pitkin was shot and then beheaded. His body was buried in a large pit just outside the compound wall, but his head was taken into the office of the niehtai, Ting Yung, as evidence of the good work of the Boxers.

All the while these horrible events were taking place a force of about thirty Chinese soldiers stood outside the gate of the Pitkin compound, knowing what was going on but taking no active part. They appeared to have remained neutral, doing absolutely nothing, which of course constituted tacit approval.

Miss Gould and Miss Morrell were taken out of the compound and into the city. Miss Gould was so frightened by the rough and brutal treatment that she fainted from shock and fear and remained in a more or less comatose condition for some time. Since she was unable to walk, they bound her hand and foot and slung her on a pole and carried her into Paotingfu, the way the Chinese carry pigs. Miss Morrell was a fearless woman of considerable moral strength, and

Forebodings in Peking

she walked. With Miss Gould being carried like an animal and Miss Morrell walking but being led by the hair, they were taken to the Chi-Sheng-An Temple in the southeast corner of the city near the wall. This was one of the headquarters of the Boxers, and here the two women were forced to remain all the long day. En route to the temple the streets had been thronged with Chinese, many of whom clutched at and tore the clothing of the women until it was in tatters. No deliberate effort was made to parade them in a nude state, nor does it appear that they were violated, in fact such is highly improbable; but they were roughly handled and knocked about on what must have seemed an endless journey.

The Chinese Christians and servants in the American Board mission compound, about ten in number, died about the same time as Mr. Pitkin and were also buried with his body.

During the day Mr. and Mrs. Bagnell, one child, and Mr. William Cooper were also brought to the Chi-Sheng-An Temple and presumably all were put through a form of examination as to their "guilt" according to the usual custom of the Boxers. Late in the afternoon, about 6 P.M., the entire party was led out of the city. Miss Gould had recovered her strength and self-possession and this time was able to walk with the others. The hands of the victims were bound and held in front of the body, the wrists raised to about the height of the neck. A rope was then tied about the wrists, passing to the rear around the neck, then to the wrists of the next person behind, then about the neck, and so on. The child was not bound but ran along clinging to her mother's dress and sobbing. The end of the rope in front was held by two men, and the missionaries were yanked along in single file, bound together like criminals and viewed by throngs of yelling Chinese as they passed through the streets and out the south gate to the southeast corner of the wall between the moat and the wall. There they met their doom; all were beheaded except the child, who was killed when speared by a Boxer. The bodies were insecurely buried in one pit, about 40 yards from the south wall and about 70 yards west of the corner.

Both compounds and graves were personally visited by Captain Grote Hutcheson, Sixth U.S. Cavalry, on October 25, 1900. Captain Hutcheson was a staff officer on the expedition from Peking to Paotingfu and back during October and November 1900. (See Chapter X.)

Chapter V

The Besieged Legations

After dark the very first evening of the siege, the Boxers and Chinese soldiers opened up with a terrible fusillade that they repeated night after night. Eventually the foreigners became somewhat accustomed to the firing and contemptuously referred to it as "the serenade." Unfortunately it was not completely ineffective, for each night some of the defenders were killed or wounded. Sorties were conducted against the assailants to force them back or to destroy their guns, and casualties usually resulted from these operations.

Sir Claude MacDonald, the minister from England, was selected to command and direct the defense because of his military experience extending over twenty-five years. He selected Mr. H. G. Squires, First Secretary of the the U.S. Legation, as his chief of staff, and the necessary committees for management of internal affairs were appointed and organized.

The military strength of the legations was as follows:

Nation	Officers	Men
United States	3	53
Austria	5	30
Great Britain	3	79
France	3	45
Germany	1	50
Japan	1	24
Russia	2	79
Italy	1	28

In addition to the above there were approximately 200 foreign civilians armed with guns of all kinds, making a total fighting strength of about 600. The Americans armed about fifty civilians with their extra guns including one Colt heavy machine gun; the

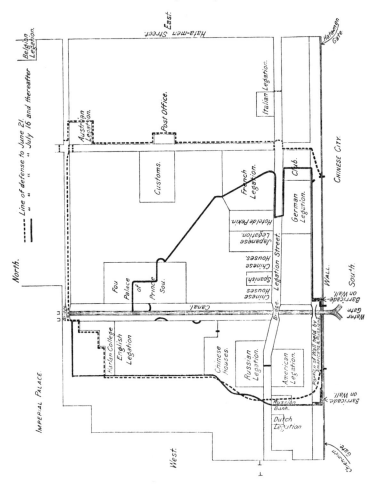

11. Lines of defense of the Legation Quarter.

British had one five-barreled Nordenfelt gun; the Italians had a 1-inch rapid-fire gun; the Austrians had a rapid-fire Maxim; and the Russians had several large-bore rifles, something like jingals, which made a very loud noise that frightened the Chinese. An old gun in an ancient foundry was loaded with pieces of scrap iron and brick and used once or twice, primarily to frighten the assailants. The Americans had about 300 rounds of ammunition per man; the Russians had about 65 per man but reloaded quite a number of brass cartridge cases; and the Germans had about 40 per man. The number of rounds possessed by the other nations is not known.

The total number of men, women, and children was about 3,500. The Christian converts rendered valuable service under the missionaries' direction in all construction works, the Catholics working principally in the Japanese legation and the Protestants on the wall. The eleven legations (Belgium, Holland, and Spain in addition to those listed above) occupied an area approximately three-quarters of a mile square. It was bounded on the south by the crenellated wall of Tartar City, which was about 40 feet high and 40 to 50 feet thick; on the north and west by the yellow wall of the Imperial City, just as high and thick but with fewer menacing fortifications; and on the east by the wall of Tartar City. Access to the great thoroughfare outside the wall was through the Ha Ta Men. A shallow canal running from north to south roughly divided the area.

The number of Chinese engaged in the siege has been conservatively estimated at about 2,000. It is known that they had four artillery guns on the Imperial wall north of the British legation, at least two guns on the Chien Men, one on the Ha Ta Men, and one at the foot of the ramp near the Ha Ta Men. Some were 3-inch modern guns, made in 1896, firing shells, others were old-fashioned types firing solid shot. The effect on their artillery reacted principally on the morale, though it also battered the barricades.

The general plan of defense was to hold a line including all the legations and that part of the Tartar Wall from the ramp immediately south of the U.S. Legation to the canal or water gate. If burned out or forced back from the outer legations and the wall, they proposed to make a final stand in the British compound. The importance of securing and holding the wall was recognized early in the defense. If it fell into the hands of the Chinese, they would be in a position to destroy almost every legation. If the legations could hold the water gate also, it would offer an easy entrance for a relief expedition. After the arrival of the marines on May 31, in addition to the guards at the legation gates, outposts were established by the Americans on Legation Street about 300 yards west and in the rear of the legation,

The Besieged Legations

by the Italians on the street just east of their legation, and by the British north of their legation on the bridge across the canal. This constituted the first step in the defenses.

Soon it became necessary to erect barricades across the streets to keep out the crowds of suspected Chinese. At first the barricades were built of old carts, wheels, and rubbish of all kinds, but afterward they were strongly reconstructed of dirt and brick. By June 13 barricades had been built by the Russians across Legation Street, by the British at their canal bridge outpost, by the French and Austrians just north of the Austrian legation, by the Italians across Legation Street at their legation, by the Germans across the street, running along the Tartar Wall and on the wall, and at numerous other locations by both the Americans and the Russians. Soon the whole of Legation Street was being fired upon from all directions, with particularly severe rifle and gunfire from the Chien Men from time to time.

In the beginning the foreigners were fired upon by small arms weapons, but the Chinese gradually moved in guns of large caliber and began to attack the foreigners with shell and round shot. Mrs. Conger, the wife of the American minister, who followed her own special brand of philosophy, regarded the pyrotechnic display of firearms as a figment of the imagination. While it was a comforting delusion, it was a little difficult for the others to regard a solid six-pound round shot as pure fancy. Nevertheless Mrs. Conger's equanimity helped the women and children to maintain a hopeful and cheerful attitude despite their confinement and hardships.

Edwin Conger was an old soldier as well as a diplomat. He had fought in the Civil War and marched with General Sherman's troops from Atlanta to the sea. He met the trials and tribulations of the siege with both cool judgment and fortitude. And while the men fought or took their posts on guard duty, the women made many thousand sandbags to strengthen their fortifications. Food, of course, was a major problem. The legationers subsisted on the coarsest bread and the poorest meat. Usually it was horse meat, with occasional mule meat for variety. Even so the ration was so small that each individual was allowed only three ounces a day. Milk was a special luxury, since no fresh or condensed milk could be obtained, and six or seven babies died from the lack of it.

The Chinese quickly recognized the value that a position on the wall south of the legation district would give them and started to advance from the Chien Men. If the foreigners were going on the wall at all, they had to do so before the Chinese reached and held the ramp. Accordingly a party of U.S. Marines, 15 Germans, and

10 Frenchmen, under Captain Myers, was sent up the wall by the east ramp with instructions to force the Chinese back and secure themselves behind a barricade. Sharp firing by the Chinese in the houses at the base of the west ramp made it necessary to use the ditch to approach the wall and for all future communications. On reaching the top of the ramp the party encountered Chinese fire from the top of the wall and up the west ramp. To protect themselves they constructed a barricade at the top of the east ramp. A barricade at the top of the west ramp would have made their position more tenable and prevented the Chinese from reaching the top of the wall by the west ramp. It would have avoided the necessity of later storming—at very great risk—a barricade constructed at that very place by the Chinese. Considering the fire up the ramp and along the wall, the difficulty of building any sort of barricade with Chinese labor can be imagined, but the necessity for erecting a barricade quickly was apparent.

A wall and a ditch were constructed, principally by the Christian Chinese, in order to maintain communication between the English and Japanese legations. This construction was very difficult because there was quite a little water in the canal, and the British had been forced to withdraw their outpost on the bridge, leaving an open field of fire from the Chinese on the Imperial City wall. The Chinese burned the buildings to the north and west of the Japanese legation, driving the defenders back on June 22. The next day the British advanced their defensive position on the north and burned the buildings sheltering the Chinese adjacent to the Mongol Market.

Two weeks later the British advanced to a better defensive position. Ditches were dug behind the walls of the British legation for the purpose of intercepting any Chinese mines and were effective in preventing the successful completion of a Chinese mining operation in the northwest corner. Western diplomats were confident that the Chinese veneration for learning, tradition, and beauty would prevent them from damaging their own buildings—which included the ancient Hanlin Library. But the diplomatic judgment was wrong: The Chinese systematically fired building after building. Soon the area was a raging inferno; even the trees were blazing like torches. Little more than six feet separated the British legation, on whose security the defense of the entire quarter depended, from the conflagration. All the women, including the ministers' wives, and children passed buckets of water from hand to hand to assist in fighting the flames. Of all the enemy's weapons, the firebrand was the most dreaded. Only at the last moment did the direction of the wind change, and the worst of the danger was over. But the Chinese in their attempt to

The Besieged Legations

burn out the British had sacrificed the Hanlin Library, which had housed one of the oldest and richest library collections in the world. Except for a few books and manuscripts picked up at random, the ancient treasure was destroyed. Although no complete record of the Library's holding is available, it was known to have contained a 23,000-volume encyclopedia, commissioned by the second Emperor of the Ming Dynatsy, which was completed in 1407 by more than 2,000 scholars. The work included historical, philosophical, classical, and literary monographs embracing astronomy, geometry, sciences, medicine, and the arts.

All attempts by the Chinese to burn out other legations failed, but it was not long before all the buildings outside the defensive perimeter had been destroyed by fire. The danger of a wholesale Chinese-set conflagration of legation buildings was now greatly diminished. There were other hazards, however. At the French legation the Chinese successfully planted and exploded a mine that burned the minister's house and those adjoining, and the French were nearly forced to abandon their legation. The barricade on the wall behind the American legation had scarcely been completed when the Chinese from the Chien Men turned their guns on it, battered it down, and forced the defenders off the wall. The position was retaken, and the barricades were strengthened and extended halfway into the bastion. The Chinese continued advancing along the wall under the shelter of barricades constructed principally at night until they had built a strong obstruction across the wall and the top of the west ramp. By breaching the wall on the north side they established communication by the ramp to positions behind the barricade.

All the while there was continuous firing from the wall on the U.S. Legation. Observing that because of the thickness of the defender's barricade and the smallness of their loopholes they could fire only straight to the front, the Chinese extended the right side of their barrier, curving it to the front so close to the foreigners that they could throw stones at them. On July 1 the Chinese attacked from the Ha Ta Men and drove the Germans from the barricade on the wall and into the street below. Two days later the Chinese had built a strong barricade on the wall, so it was obvious that the position on the wall behind the American legation was the only hope of retaining the wall—and that position was being attacked from both sides. If the position was to be held, shelter from hostile fire coming from two opposite directions had to be provided.

At 2 A.M. on July 3, Captain Myers and 53 men (15 U.S. Marines, 23 British, and 15 Russians) charged the Chinese barricade—

the Americans and British attacking the center and right flank, and the Germans the left flank—with the hope of cutting off any escape and preventing assistance from the ramp. Within ten minutes the position was taken at a loss of 2 Americans killed and 1 wounded. Captain Myers was wounded in the leg when he ran into a spear lying on the ground. A number of the Chinese killed had been thrown over the wall, but 27 bodies remained to be buried. After Captain Myers was wounded, Captain Hall took command on the wall.

Under his direction the defenders built a strong barricade on the wall, extending it to the south side of the bastion. They also put a doorway in their wall and dug a small ditch for sheltered communications. Scarcely had they fortified themselves from attack by the Chinese on the Chien Men side than they began operating toward the Ha Ta Men for possession of the water gate. After the night attack of July 3 the Chinese began building a tower of brick from which they could fire over the defenders' barricade when they were moving toward the Ha Ta Men and from which they could fire directly into the American legation. A ditch 10 feet deep across the wall at the tower and a tunnel 6 feet long had been dug, showing their intention to undermine the defenders.

The defenders sent out a party of Christian converts to build a barricade to the east, but they were intimidated by the firing and built only a few feet. A second party was sent out under a marine corporal, but they built only a small segment of little appreciable advantage. Finally, under Captain Hall, two barricades and a communication ditch for shelter were built on July 12, 13, and 15. In constructing these barricades the working party advanced, built the obstruction as quickly as possible, then dug the ditch. Securely fortified in this position, the defenders held command of the water gate and canal and kept the Chinese off until the relief column arrived on August 14 to raise the siege.

At the outset of the siege the legationers had expected it to last only a few days, but when they learned from a Chinese runner-messenger that the Seymour Relief Expedition had been driven back, they realized that the siege might last considerably longer. For the beseiged, hemmed in on all sides and receiving no information from the outside world, hope was rapidly giving way to despair. When the food supply was depleted to a two-day ration of horse meat and a two-week supply of bread, they were face to face with starvation. Then on the night of August 14 a guard rushed into Mr. Conger's bedroom shouting, "They are coming—the relief army—I hear the guns!" The word was spread. Soon men, women, and children came into the courtyard to listen with the greatest joy and thanksgiving to the music of friendly firearms on the outer walls of the enclave. Women wept and threw themselves into each other's arms, while the men moved about grasping hands with emotion that ran too deep for words.

During the siege of Peking a total of 67 men were killed and 167 of the foreign legations' personnel were wounded. The one American civilian wounded was said to have been shot while in the act of looting. There were two or three determined attacks by the Chinese, one just prior to the arrival of the relief column, but during the greater part of the siege the firing was desultory and individual. Snipers and sharpshooters under cover caused considerable trouble and were greatly feared, though there were not many of them. There was evidence of heavy rifle fire around the legation buildings but little of artillery fire. It was reported that 2,000 shots were fired in one week, but poor quality guns and poor marksmanship, and perhaps such outdated Chinese guns as jingals used as artillery pieces, accounted for the little damage caused by enemy shelling.

Considering the number of Chinese actually engaged in the attack and the thousands more that were available, the situation of the legation quarter near the Tartar Wall, and the advantageous positions of the Chinese, it is difficult to find any military reason for the failure of the Chinese to exterminate the foreigners. Their half-hearted offensive may have been due to cowardice or to a lack of intent really to destroy the legations and kill their inhabitants. The absence of the necessary will may be explained by a disinclination of the Chinese government to oppose the legation personnel except insofar as to divert attention from itself.

Although much has been told and written about the siege of the legation quarter, it can be repeated that the defenders fought bravely, endured many, many hardships, and suffered untold miseries in anticipation of the barbarous death which certainly seemed inevitable.

The Siege of the Pietang

The Pietang, or French mission, was situated just within the west wall of the Imperial City and therefore was entirely separated from the legation quarter. Here all were Catholics, against whom the Chinese were particularly active because of the deep roots Catholicism was putting down in China due to their methods directed toward the rearing, educating, and Christianizing of Chinese children. Within the large compound were located all the buildings pertaining to such an institution—cathedral, convent, dwelling houses, orphanage, schoolrooms, etc. The regular contingent consisted of 600 persons, including priests, nuns, Christian Chinese men, women, and children; but the influx of refugees just prior to the siege swelled the number to nearly 3,000. One year's supplies for 600 people had fortunately just been received, and as soon as the converts and refugees began to pour in, an effort was made to obtain more supplies; but Chinese interference prevented this.

Thirty French soldiers were sent on June 1 to defend the mission, augmented by 10 Italian soldiers on June 10. Immediately upon their arrival work was begun to build barricades, dig communication trenches, reinforce walls, and build a small bombproof shelter. On June 19 the Chinese opened fire, killing 47 persons and burning one house. The last communication with the other legations was on June 21. Monsignors Favier and Jardin, priests of the mission, directed the defense. The plan was to hold the outer wall as long as possible and, if forced back, to make a final stand in the cathedral, which was loopholed for defense. In addition to 2 officers and 41 soldiers, 10 Chinese Christians were armed with the spare guns on hand. The French had 300 rounds of ammunition per man and the Italians 90, a few cartridges were reloaded, and some spears were made but never used.

The Chinese were roughly estimated at 2,000 with about 22 artillery guns, some of which were Krupps. Their artillery fire was terrific at times, although not very damaging. Beginning on July 24 it was continuous for three days; 580 shots were fired on the first day, 355 on the second, and 255 on the third. Then firing ceased for about eight days, and thereafter it was desultory until the very end, when heavy fire opened up again.

Rifle fire was directed against the defenders from all directions. The buildings, especially the cathedral, showed the effect of heavy rifle fire but not much artillery fire. Few lives were lost from gunshots. The Chinese artillery guns were inferior and the marksmanship was worse. Occasionally the Chinese would launch an attack, but a few volleys from the outposts would stop them. The defenders made a sortie out the south gate and captured an artillery piece, but since there was no ammunition for it, it was useless to them.

The Chinese attempted numerous mine-planting operations. Some were discovered but others exploded. In one instance three small mines exploded, killing one man and damaging one building; at another time a mine blew up and killed 1 Catholic brother and the 23 Christians working under him as they were digging a trench along the wall in the northwest corner. The defenders planted a mine themselves in the northeast corner, which was being continually at-

The Besieged Legations

tacked, but they had insufficient powder for it. At 6 A.M. on August 12 the Chinese set off a mine that left a crater 80 feet in diameter and 30 feet deep. The explosion was terrific, completely demolishing adjacent buildings and walls and killing 5 Italian soldiers, 1 brother, about 20 Chinese men and 50 children. The most serious attack was made on the south gate—the Chinese fired from rifle pits in the northwest corner, and artillery guns fired from various positions on the north. The arrival of the Japanese and French troops on August 16 dispersed the Chinese and raised the siege.

During the siege 11 military personnel were killed and 12 wounded. In addition, about 44 adult Chinese Christians and 50 children were killed, and about 250 adults and as many children died of starvation. Mules, burros, ponies, etc., were used for meat, and even leaves from the trees were boiled for food. On hand at the end for the approximately 2,400 people remaining were only one mule and 400 pounds of grain—a little over 2½ ounces each. And this frugal allowance was available because of the 500 deaths from starvation. To enable them to keep up the defense as long as possible, soldiers had been given a little larger ration than the others.

The comparatively few deaths from gunshots among soldiers continually fighting, the fact that 1,500 rounds of ammunition remained out of the original 10,000, and that after a siege of more than two months this handful of soldiers withstood the attacks, shows that the best possible defense dispositions were made and exercised. Further, it accords to the soldiers an enviable claim to one of the noblest and bravest defenses known to history.

In retrospect the following facts seem to indicate the complicity of the Imperial government and the Boxers in the attack on the legations:

(1) The attack was made by Imperial troops.

(2) The Chinese barricades were mounted everywhere with flags bearing the name and designation of regular Chinese officers and their commands, and captured men and arms belonged to the Chinese army.

(3) Decrees were issued organizing, arming, provisioning, and paying the Boxers; appointing Prince Chuang and Kang Yi to their command; urging members of the Imperial family to be no less patriotic than the Boxers; and mentioning princes and ministers in command of Boxers.

(4) Viceroy Yu Lu ordered provisions and firearms distributed among the Boxers.

(5) Whenever the Chinese government desired to communicate with the legation ministers, the firing would cease for a while.

Thus, although there appears to be but little doubt that the government was involved, it might be stated in its defense that it would have been very unpopular with the Chinese people had it not encouraged and abetted the movement against the foreigners and even might have been overthrown by its own people.

Chapter VI

The Seymour Relief Expedition and the Taku Forts

Determined to protect American lives and property endangered by the widespread disorder in the Chinese Empire, Admiral Kempff, in command of all U.S. war vessels north of Hong Kong, arrived at Taku on May 28, 1900. Other governments had taken similar action to protect their interests, and by June 4 the international fleet at Taku totaled 25 warships. Men from these ships were to be landed to go to Peking as guards for the various legations.

As early as February 17 Jas. W. Ragsdale, the U.S. consul in Tientsin, expressed his concern to the Assistant Secretary, in his dispatch No. 44, over the growth and activities of the Boxers. The Boxer infection reached the native city of Tientsin in May, and by the 27th of the month the situation had grown so alarming that at 9 P.M. the consul sent the following message to Admiral Kempff aboard the U.S. Flagship *Newark:*

Sir: Part of railway to Paotingfu destroyed by Boxers last evening. Three stations already burned. Destruction of main line to Pekin threatened. Workshops and godowns at several stations from Pekin already destroyed. Boxers are in control and stations deserted by agents and employees. Viceroy promises to send troops to-morrow morning, but I have doubts as to their reliability. There is great uneasiness here amongst the foreigners, and the situation is most serious. Can't you land a force of marines with Maxim or quick-firing guns? If so, bring by rail if permitted, otherwise by river.

This message was telegraphed to Tangku and sent out by a tug, reaching the Admiral at 4 A.M. on the 28th. In response to this plea immediate arrangements were made to send troops.

On June 3 Admiral Kempff landed 50 men with the consent of the Chinese government, and two days later 50 additional men were disembarked for the protection of Americans in both Peking and

Tientsin. He then requested the Secretary of the Navy in Washington to provide additional ships and men to meet the emergency.

By this time the Boxers were overrunning the country from Tientsin to Peking and beyond. Murders and depredations were reported on every side. From Tientsin on June 5 came the news that the Boxers were closing in on the city, which was practically under arms, and that even larger bodies of troops were moving from beyond Yangtsun to attack it. The Chinese army, under General Nieh, which was presumably opposing the Boxers, was defeated by them in one encounter, and the soldiers said it was useless to fight Boxers since they could not be killed by bullets. On June 9 the foreigners were greatly alarmed not only because they expected an immediate attack, but in addition an urgent message was received from the ministers in Peking asking for assistance. The senior naval commanders at once organized a force composed of all available men from the various warships to start immediately for Peking under the command of Vice Admiral Sir Edward H. Seymour, K.C.B.

The international armada anchored off the Taku bar was about 12

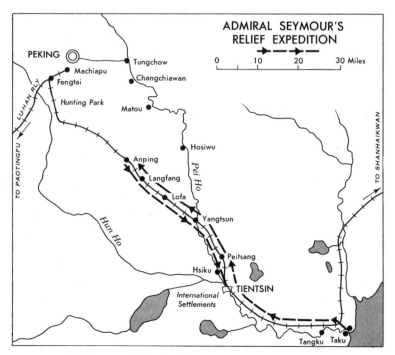

12. *Route of Admiral Seymour's Relief Expedition.*

The Seymour Relief Expedition and the Taku Forts 91

miles off shore. Troops making up the Peking force had to be transferred to destroyers, lighters, gunboats, and shallow-draft vessels that ferried them past the Taku forts guarding the mouth of the Pei Ho (North River) to the small river port of Tangku. From there they traveled by railway to Tientsin, 80 miles from Peking.

The first train from Tangku carried 300 British, 112 Americans, 40 Italians, and 25 Austrians. Starting about 6 A.M. on June 10, it reached Tientsin at 7:30 A.M. and left there two hours later, proceeding without opposition beyond Yangtsun, near a camp of 4,000 Chinese troops commanded by General Nieh. At 3:30 P.M. it reached a point a few miles from Lofa where it had to be halted to make repairs to the railroad, and it remained there overnight. Two more trains joined the expedition there, increasing the total force to 1,798 officers and men: English 905, German 450, Russian 112, American 112, French 100, Japanese 54, Italian 40, and Austrian 25.

Early the next morning, June 11, the trains pulled into the station, where the engines were watered. A fourth train, carrying 200 Russians and 58 French troops, also arrived in the morning, making the expedition total 2,056. The four trains departed a little before noon, leaving a guard at Lofa of 1 officer and 30 men, later reinforced to 60, to protect the line. From Lofa the expedition advanced without special incident until it reached a point about three miles from Langfang (halfway to Peking), where the leading train was attacked by Boxers who had first tried and failed to cut off an advance railway repair party. They then attacked in skirmish order and were soon repulsed by rifle fire, leaving about 35 Chinese dead.

The next day, June 12, as soon as the track was repaired, the trains moved forward and arrived at Langfang. From there on it was found that the railway line was considerably damaged, and that the damage was recent and had evidently been done by Boxers who were operating just ahead of the relief force. Since several days would have to be spent at Langfang repairing bridges, track, etc., a party of 3 officers and 44 men was sent to Anping, about 13 miles beyond, to hold that station and prevent further destruction of the railway line. The party reached Anping the next morning and was subjected to repeated attacks that were repulsed with heavy losses to the Boxers estimated, with those previously killed, to be about 150. With its ammunition running low, the detachment wisely returned to the main body, rejoining it on the afternoon of June 13. Another party of 60 men went out that same afternoon with the same objective, but it failed to accomplish its mission and returned on June 15. However, it killed about 25 Boxers without any casualties on its side.

On the morning of June 14 the outposts at Langfang ran in, closely pursued by Boxers in great numbers who made a determined rush on the front of the train then standing alongside a well. With great courage they advanced in loose formation under a withering fire. Some even managed to reach the train before being killed, although about 100 died before they retreated. In this encounter the Italian contingent lost five men. They were on outpost duty near a deserted village that concealed the approach of the enemy until it was too late for them to escape.

In the afternoon a messenger reported an attack on the Lofa station, and reinforcements were sent at once to assist the guard. The worst of the fighting was over by the time they arrived; however, the reinforcements harassed the retreating Boxers, who left behind about 100 dead and 2 small cannon. Two British seamen were wounded in the skirmish, one of whom died afterwards.

The difficulties of the expedition began to multiply rapidly. Repairs to the railroad line had to be made under the protection of strong guards, only to be destroyed again by the Boxers both in front of and behind them. On June 16 the rail line to Tientsin was found to be broken, and telegraph communication had been cut off since the 13th by the numerous bands that infested the country. The determined enemy opposition encountered by the relief force had so delayed its advance that provisions and ammunition were running low. It was believed that they could not go by railroad any farther than Anping, where they would then have to march overland; and this would not be possible without some means of transporting the supplies. They were also cut off from their base at Tientsin and had no knowledge of what was happening there.

A few days earlier, Admiral Seymour had endeavored to send orders to Tientsin directing that junks, provisions, and ammunition be sent to Yangtsun, where the railroad crossed the river, for the purpose of making it a base from which to proceed north to Tungchow by water. He then planned to march to Peking, a distance of about 13 miles. None of his messengers succeeded in getting through, however. On the morning of June 17 train No. 1 reached Yangtsun after considerable difficulty and delay. The station and water tanks had been entirely destroyed, and the rails had buckled from burnt railroad ties to such an extent that it was impossible to repair the damage with the equipment at hand. Since it was impracticable to advance by rail, and since there was a possibility that the isolated trains might be attacked and destroyed separately, messages were sent to Lofa and Langfang recalling trains 2, 3, and 4.

In the afternoon of June 18 train No. 3 arrived from Lofa, and later in the evening trains 2 and 4 came in from Langfang. The latter

The Seymour Relief Expedition and the Taku Forts 93

had been attacked unexpectedly about 2:30 that afternoon by a force estimated at 5,000 men, including cavalry, large numbers of whom were armed with magazine rifles of the latest models. Captured banners showed they belonged to the army of General Tung Fu Hsiang, who commanded the Chinese troops in the hunting park outside Peking, thus showing that Chinese Imperial troops were being employed to defeat the expedition. This army was composed of especially picked men, 10,000 strong, commanded from the palace. They were reported to be well armed but poorly trained. The attack was made in front and on both flanks, but it was repelled with great loss to the Chinese. However, when the assailants saw the relief troops retire toward the trains, they rallied and attacked again. They were driven off with even greater losses than before and finally retreated. The Chinese lost about 400 killed in this encounter; 6 of the allies were killed and 48 wounded.

The relief force was now reunited at Yangtsun, and on June 19 the commanders of the different units held a conference at which it was decided to abandon the trains and withdraw to Tientsin, marching by the north bank of the river. The American contingent, under the command of Captain B. H. McCalla, U.S.M.C., was given the advance. An attempt to establish friendly relations and procure supplies from the town authorities was unsuccessful, due to their fear of the vengeance of the Boxers who were in the neighborhood in force.

Preparations for the retreat were quickly made; the wounded were loaded into four junks seized the day before, and the expedition pulled out at 3 P.M. After a short march of 2½ miles it bivouacked for the night. An early start was made the next day, June 20. Progress, governed by the speed of the junks that were manned with unskilled soldier crewmen, was necessarily slow and was further delayed by continuous fighting to force a way through a succession of villages that had to be taken by rifle fire or with the bayonet. The bayonet was most effective, and the cheers and shouting of the troops in their foreign tongues seemed to intimidate the Chinese, who would fall back without waiting to engage in personal hand-to-hand conflict. About 8 miles were covered in the day's march.

The march was resumed at 7:30 the following morning and was marked by stiffer opposition from the enemy. Soon after the column moved out, a body of about 200 Chinese cavalry was seen in the distance to the left of the advance. At first they were thought to be Cossacks, but as they approached nearer to reconnoiter, they were identified as Chinese. A few well-directed shrapnel bursts from the 9-pounder made them withdraw to a distance that they maintained for the rest of the day, although they fired a few shots from time to time. After the cavalry had been driven off, the enemy opened up with a field gun. This was repeated at intervals during the day, but whenever the position of the Chinese gun could be located, its firing was stopped by the allies' 9-pounder, at least temporarily. The advance continued through the villages along the river and through the town of Peitsang, opposed every foot of the way. At 6 P.M. the enemy was found in a strong position from which he could not be dislodged during the remaining hours of daylight. A halt was called while the commanders considered possible courses of action. They had moved only 6 miles during the day.

It was decided that a night march would offer the best chance for the column to get through, so after a few hours' rest the party started out about 1 A.M. on June 22. Resistance was encountered early in the march, but the troops struggled on, and at 4 A.M. arrived opposite the Imperial armory near Hsiku on the opposite bank of the river. Unexpected heavy rifle and gunfire was opened up on the column. Fortunately cover was available in a nearby village and behind the river bank, both of which were taken advantage of immediately. When the rear of the column had come up, and the junks carrying the wounded had been placed in the best-protected locations, an attack was made on the armory with rifle fire on the river front. Some Chinese were killed and others driven from their guns. Two parties were dispatched, one above and one below, that crossed the river unobserved and captured the armory by assault.

The main body and the wounded crossed over in the afternoon and occupied the building. A strong attempt by the Chinese to retake the armory during the afternoon was defeated, with the Chinese suffering heavy losses. The allies also suffered severely; among their dead was Commander Buchholtz, Imperial German Navy, whose death was a blow not only to the Germans, but also to the whole force. About 6 A.M. the next morning, the 23rd, the Chinese again attacked the armory and again were successfully repulsed.

Inside the building the allied troops found about 15 tons of rice, a number of guns, large quantities of ammunition, and war matériel of the latest models. The situation of the allied forces was now much improved, but many difficulties still confronted them. The necessity of carrying the 230 wounded prevented them from forcing their way to Tientsin because practically the whole command would be required for the task, leaving very few men available for fighting. Repeated attempts to get word of their predicament into Tientsin had been futile, since the country had been so closely watched.

On June 23 a native courier did manage to get through. He had been captured by Boxers and tied to a tree at one point, but since he had destroyed his message before being caught, nothing incriminating was found on him. Finally released, he made his way with great difficulty and cunning through the lines at Tientsin. A Chinese soldier, who was wounded and captured by the allies while trying to enter the armory, said that General Nieh's army was very discouraged by their failures, and that attempts to retake the armory were made with 25 battalions that would normally have a strength of 500 men, but at the time were manned only to a strength of 300 to 400 each. With the armory occupied, the defenders maintained aggressive gunfire on a Boxer stronghold nearby and on a fort down the river, using their captured weapons to good advantage. This prevented the Chinese from giving the allies further trouble.

In the meantime the situation at Tientsin and Taku had been radically changed. The departure of the Seymour Relief Expedition on June 10 left Tientsin with only a small force for defense in case of attack. By June 13 the Boxers had taken possession of the native city and almost surrounded it, cutting off all communication with the relief expedition and threatening communications with the base at Taku.

On June 14 word was received at Taku from the consuls at Tientsin that all railway cars and rolling stock at Tangku were to be sent up the line for the purpose of transporting a Chinese army to Tangku, and orders were given at once to the allied vessels in the Pei Ho to prevent any rolling stock from being moved, and to oppose with force any action of that kind. By the evening of the next day, June 15, it was learned that the mouth of the river was protected by electric mines, that the forts at Taku were being provisioned with supplies and ammunition, and that reinforcements were being brought in. The naval commanders reached an agreement at a conference the following day and notified the viceroy of Chihli at Tientsin that in view of the danger to the allied forces marching to Peking and to those at Tientsin, they (the commanders) would occupy the Taku forts temporarily at 2 A.M. on June 17.

The time fixed by the allies for taking possession of the forts was set so that they could be bombarded at 4 A.M. if they had not surrendered. But at 12:50 A.M. on June 17 the Chinese in the forts anticipated the strategy of the allies by opening fire simultaneously from every gun that could be trained on the ships. This action was said to have been taken at the express direction of the Dowager Empress, who regarded the notice of the commanders as a declaration of war on the Chinese government and believed the dismemberment of the Empire had been agreed on by the world powers. If fire was opened by the direction of the Empress, it proved that the Chinese had telegraphic communication with Peking after it had been closed to foreigners.

The allies' plan for the attack had been agreed upon and their vessels were already in their assigned places, except the *Iltis* and the *Lion,* when the forts opened fire. To enable the *Iltis* and *Lion* to take their stations with safety, the English torpedo boat destroyers *Fame* and *Whiting* were ordered to capture four Imperial Chinese destroyers lying at the dockyard between Taku and Tangku. This was swiftly accomplished. A few Chinese were killed and wounded on one of their destroyers, but there were no casualties among the English.

The Taku forts were described as three forts of the Chinese type, armed with numerous cannon of different systems and calibers, and poorly placed. The forts were constructed of soft coast mud that dries in time and was called in derision by Europeans "harveyized mud." Sometimes it crumbled to pieces upon the discharge of its own guns. Admiral Kempff did not agree with this last assertion. In a report of the bombardment he stated that "the forts being of thick mud and grass adobe, were but little damaged by the gunfire, although they received a host of projectiles." They were known as the North, Northwest, and South Forts. The two former were on the north and the latter on the south side of the entrance to the river.

The movements of the gunboats were directed by the Russian, Captain Dobrovolsky, of the *Bohr.* Those joining in the attack were the *Koreetz, Guilak,* and *Bohr,* Russian; the *Iltis,* German; *Lion,* French; and the *Algerine,* British. Since the engines of the Japanese gunboat were disabled, she was moored near Tangku to protect the railroad station there.

The plans of the allies included a land attack to be conducted by Commander Craddock of the British Navy. The forces involved were as follows:

> British: 23 officers and 298 men; Commander Craddock, H.M.S. *Alacrity.*
> Japanese: 4 officers and 240 men; Commander Hattori, I.J.S. *Kasagi.*
> German: 3 officers and 130 men; Commander Pohl, H.I.M.S. *Hansa.*
> Russian: 2 officers and 157 men; Lieutenant Stankewitch.
> Italian: 1 officer and 24 men; Lieutenant J. Tanca, I.M.S. *Calabria.*

Austrian: 2 officers and 20 men; Lieutenant Ernt. Tatni, *Zenta.* *Total*: 904 officers and men.

The fire from the forts was quickly returned by the gunboats and continued through the night. At daylight the firing increased in intensity and inflicted greater damage to the forts of the Chinese. The British landing party was put ashore from the *Algerine* after the firing commenced and joined the others who had marched from Tangku to a rendezvous previously agreed on. It was planned that after an effective bombardment, the Northwest Fort should be attacked first, then the North Fort, and finally the long string of fortifications on the south bank of the river known as the South Fort.

The attack on the Northwest Fort was to be an assault at the west gate. After forcing it or scaling the wall, an entrance to the inner fort was to be located and attacked. The first advance was made about 3 A.M., but the line was halted about 1,000 yards from the fort and then retired a short distance to gain cover, pending further bombardment by the gunboats. So far, little damage had been done to the fort; all its guns were still in action. The commanders agreed that an attack then would result in a serious and unnecessary loss of life. Fire by the gunboats on the Northwest Fort had ceased on the request of Commander Craddock about the time preparations were being made for the first advance, but was kept up on the other forts. It was resumed on the Northwest Fort by the *Algerine* and *Iltis* on the receipt of his second message to Commander Stewart of the *Algerine,* who relayed it to the other vessel by boat. This was about 3:45 A.M. and, with daylight, the fire was more accurate and effective. About 4:30 A.M. the heavy guns of the Northwest Fort had been silenced; preparations for the final attack were then made.

When the line had previously retired, a British detachment had remained under cover of a small rise in the ground about 300 yards to the front. They were joined by the Russians, who took a position on the left, shortly before the main assault. The Italians were in loose formation on the right flank, slightly in the rear—a military road prevented their moving into the line. The other forces and the remainder of the British were in close support. All moved out promptly when the advance was ordered. When the charge was sounded, the Japanese marines, who were with the support units in columns along the road, ran quickly to the front, led by Captain Hattori. They raced abreast of the English across the intervening yards to the west gate, and together they scaled the parapets.

Captain Hattori was the first man in and helped Commander Craddock climb the wall. Shortly afterward the Japanese officer was killed. The inner gate was forced by allied rifle fire, and the allies were able to take complete possession of the fort. The other defenses of Taku were taken with little opposition. The Chinese abandoned the Northwest Fort by way of a protected passage leading to the North Fort, which they later abandoned without a fight. The South Fort was captured two hours later. Its garrison fled after the explosion of a powder magazine that was hit by shells from the gunboats. As a measure of prudence, they were not pursued.

The casualties among the allied land forces included 1 warrant officer and 6 men wounded among the British. The Japanese had lost the courageous Captain Hattori and 2 men killed, 6 men wounded, 2 of whom died later. The bodies of 450 Chinese were found in the Northwest Fort; later a Chinese stated that about 50 bodies had been thrown into the moat. Of the naval vessels the Russian *Guilak* suffered the most; 10 men were killed, 2 officers and 47 men were wounded. Most of these casualties were caused by a shell that penetrated one of the ship's smaller powder magazines and exploded some of the charges in it. The vessel was also damaged by shots that penetrated the hull into the engine room. The *Iltis* also sustained severe damage, and the captain and 30 men were wounded and 8 men were killed. The German *Iltis* and its commander received unstinted praise for conspicuous and gallant service in the official reports of the British naval commanders. The *Lion* had 1 man killed; the *Koreetz*, 2 officers and several men killed and wounded; British losses were also small.

After the operation, all available men were landed from the fleet. They occupied the forts and placed them in as good a state of defense as was possible, not overlooking the likelihood of a night attack or assaults by a vast number of Boxers. The British garrisoned the Northwest Fort, the Japanese the North Fort, and the Russians and Germans jointly occupied the South Fort.

A series of seven old forts extended along the Pei Ho (river) from the seacoast to Tientsin. The most important was the Singchen, about 13 miles above Tangku, which was armed with large-caliber modern guns. But an expedition sent out on June 26 found the fort was abandoned and returned after disabling the guns and destroying a large amount of ammunition. This was a break for the allies because the fort commanded both the river and the Tientsin road. If properly manned and operated, it could have made travel on the river extremely dangerous and difficult.

In the absence of specific instructions from his superiors, Admiral Kempff was unwilling to engage in an act of war against China. As a result the U.S.S. *Monocacy* took no active part in the bombardment and remained moored at her berth near the railroad station, giving shelter and protection to many frightened foreigners during the night. Notwithstanding her inaction, the vessel was fired on many times during the night and struck once by a Chinese shell that damaged the vessel and two of her boats. Luckily there were no casualties. Commander Wise at first thought this might have been due to wild shooting, but was later convinced that the ship was an intentional target. He therefore steamed out of range to a safe position several miles up the river behind the bend at about 5 o'clock. Less than an hour later the gunfire slackened, and the Japanese flag was joyfully observed to be flying over one of the forts. At that point Wise returned to his berth.

Considerable regret and indignation was later felt and expressed in the United States that our forces had not joined in the attacks on the forts. These feelings were shared by the officers and men of the *Monocacy,* who would have rejoiced in being able to give "her ancient smooth bores a last chance."

The reduction of the forts was an essential step toward the safe progress of any relief expedition and was justified by subsequent events. Admiral Kempff no longer hesitated to join wholeheartedly with the allies in all measures deemed necessary for the protection of the foreigners. He represented to the Navy Department in Washington that the Chinese government was paralyzed and in sympathy with the Boxer outbreak; that the occupation of the forts was justified; that the firing of the Chinese on the *Monocacy* was an act of war, her pacific character being known; and that it was necessary to join with the other powers for common defense and security, and for the honor of the country. His course was promptly approved, and he was directed to act concurrently with the other powers according to his best judgment.

Having secured their base at Taku, the most urgent task that faced the allies was to reopen the way to Tientsin and relieve the foreigners beseiged in that city.

On June 19, the day after the bombardment, Major L.W.T. Waller, U.S. Marine Corps, reached Taku with 5 officers and 131 men of the Marine Corps with orders to move forward with the first relief column. The next day he went to Tangku and, assisted by Commander Wise, got a train together and proceeded up the railroad, taking a construction car with him. By hard work he managed to repair the road and reach a position about 18 miles out, where he overtook a Russian party of about 400 men. Here the road was impassable, and both parties bivouacked for the night, agreeing that the position should be held until reinforcements came up. Very early the next morning the Russian commander told Major Waller that he would push on and try to get into Tientsin to aid in its defense. This was against the judgment of the American commander, who thought that the chances were very slim for pushing through the Chinese force with only 530 men and no guns. Nevertheless, he decided to make the attempt; the 3-inch rifle, which had proved defective, was disabled and rolled into the river; and the little party of Americans followed closely after the Russians on their march toward the beleaguered city.

A detachment of marines, commanded by Lieutenant Powell, was in the advance with a Colt gun. It proceeded without opposition until 7 A.M. to a point opposite the Imperial arsenal, where the enemy opened a light fire from the flank that was quickly silenced. A few minutes later they encountered a heavy front and flank fire from an intrenched force of from 1,500 to 2,000 that proved too strong for the small attacking force, who were compelled to retire. The Colt gun was continuously in action under heavy fire from the Chinese until all but one of the detachment and Lieutenant Powell lay dead. Having jammed several times, the gun was disabled, and Lieutenant Powell abandoned it. The allies retired, fighting as they fell back, to a point 4 miles in the rear of their bivouac of the night before.

The marines succeeded in carrying off their wounded but had to leave their dead behind. The news of this conflict became known in the United States through Admiral Kempff's dispatch "that in ambush near Tientsin, on the 21st, 4 of Waller's command were killed and 7 wounded," and created a deep impression. They were the first losses of Americans in actual fighting known to have occurred, and the serious nature of the conflict began to be understood. Waller's report contained nothing about an ambuscade, but the sudden intense fire from so large a force, and the abandonment of the dead and the only remaining gun certainly indicated conditions closely resembling a surprise.

The determined resistance to the allied advance showed that a much larger force would be required before it could be overcome—and it arrived that afternoon in the form of Russian, English, and other troops. The British had arrived at Taku on June 21 on the *Terrible,* landing immediately and starting for the front a few hours later; but their progress was delayed by the derailment and overturning of two of the leading trucks, and by the necessity for making repairs along the route from time to time. The force consisted of 7 officers and 327 men of the Royal Welsh Fusiliers and a naval brigade of about 150, commanded by Commander Craddock.

The Seymour Relief Expedition and the Taku Forts   101

The next day, June 22, was devoted to clearing the line of communications of the Boxers and in moving up and establishing a base of supplies at the end of the railroad, where they were joined by an additional body of Russian infantry and a field battery of 4 guns. The force by then had a strength of about 2,500 men, of whom 1,500 were Russians and the rest British, Germans, Americans, Italians, and Japanese. On the 23rd the advance began in two columns along the railroad, Russians on the right, British and Americans on the left, with Americans in the advance party. The columns moved out at 4 A.M., and three hours later the enemy was encountered about 6 miles from Tientsin. The allies attacked at once, the Chinese responding with heavy fire.

From this point the columns diverged, the Russians taking the railway station as their objective, the left column moving to attack the military school. Village after village was cleared at bayonet point. The school was not strongly held, and the enemy was soon driven out, leaving about 25 dead and wounded behind. This school was the most threatening point to the foreign settlements held by the enemy. It was taken about 1 P.M., and the beseiged fighters poured out of their intrenchments to greet their rescuers as they crossed the river. The right column had also been successful and occupied the railway about the same time. The losses were: Russians, 4 killed, 30 wounded; Americans, 1 killed, 3 wounded; British, 1 killed, 3 wounded.

After a day of much needed rest, a relief force set out on June 25 to rescue Admiral Seymour's force. Early that morning some of Seymour's men in the armory observed that one of the guns of the Chinese fort was firing toward Tientsin. To create a diversion, two guns in the armory opened fire on it, whereupon the Chinese gun turned its fire on the armory. At 6 A.M. the relief column came in sight and an hour later arrived outside the armory. It was commanded by the Russian, Colonel Shirinsky, and composed of troops of various nations, with Russians predominating.

Preparations were soon made for the return of the combined force and for the destruction of the arsenal, which contained about $15,000,000 worth of war stores and supplies. The command crossed the river in the afternoon and bivouacked on the bank for the night. The return march was commenced at 3 A.M. on the 26th. Fires were lighted immediately afterward in five different places in the armory by two English naval officers who remained behind for that purpose, rejoining the main body when their task was completed. The dense volumes of smoke and the occasional explosions seen and heard subsequently gave assurance that the destruction was reasonably successful.

The whole command arrived at Tientsin about 9 A.M. without further incident. The wounded were cared for at once, and the various detachments rejoined their own forces.

The expedition had failed to achieve its objective—the rescue of the legation in Peking—but the severe losses suffered by the Chinese in their repeated attacks must have impaired their morale. The foreigners had proved that the Boxers were not invulnerable, and thus the task was made a little easier for the larger and better-equipped force that afterwards succeeded. The capture and destruction of the arsenal near Hsiku, with its immense stores of war matériel, was also some compensation for the danger and casualties involved.

The total losses sustained by the relief expedition were 62 killed and 228 wounded. No reliable estimate of the number of Chinese engaged in opposing the allied forces can be given. Admiral Seymour stated that the number increased gradually until the armory near Hsiku was reached, where General Nieh's troops and the Boxers both joined in the attack. Their combined strength must have greatly outnumbered the relief expedition. The traditional courage and gallantry of the U.S. Marine Corps was exemplified in the conduct of the American force of marines under the command of Captain McCalla, whose valuable services to the expedition received special praise and recognition from the commander. In fact, all the various forces had acquitted themselves well under great difficulties.

Chapter VII

The Capture of Tientsin

Tientsin is located at the junction of the Hun Ho (better known as the Grand Canal) and the Pei Ho, 51 miles by river and 31 miles by rail from Tangku. The distance to Peking by rail was 83¾ miles. Tientsin consisted of the native walled city and suburbs so extensive that it was difficult to tell exactly where the city began or ended. The walled city was a square enclosure bounded by walls about 4,000 feet long on a side, extending in the direction of the four cardinal points of the compass. The walls were about 25 feet high and 20 feet thick at the top, faced with the dark gray brick of the country. They were very old in 1900, and the interior revetment had fallen down in many places, especially along the south face. The population of the city was reputed to be about 1,000,000, which was probably exaggerated.

The foreigners lived in the three concessions—British, French, and German—that fringed the river below the city, covering an area of somewhat less than 500 acres. These had been greatly improved and contained handsome municipal buildings, library, theater, hotels, churches, etc. An outer mud wall surrounded the concessions and the interior city. A racecourse located outside the mud wall, two or three miles southwest of the British concession, had been the scene of several conflicts between the foreigners and the Chinese.

After the departure of Admiral Seymour's Relief Expedition only a small garrison of about 600 men remained in Tientsin to protect the foreign settlement and to keep communications open. Its composition was as follows: British, 243; Germans, 110; French, 50; Austrians, 50; Japanese, 50; Americans, 43; and Italians, 40. On June 11 the garrison strength was increased by the arrival of 150 English seamen and marines, and on the 13th about 1,800 Russians with some cavalry and field guns arrived, bringing the total strength to about 2,500 men.

The Boxers and their sympathizers took advantage of the weakness of the foreigners to obstruct the forwarding of supplies and reinforcements by rail to Admiral Seymour's party. This was done by large, threatening mobs that thronged the railway station and interfered with the operations, and finally tracks were torn up and bridges destroyed, so that by June 13 communication with Seymour's expedition was cut off entirely. The day after the expedition departed from Tientsin the Chinese began to close their shops and leave the settlement, evidently anticipating trouble. By June 15 the Boxers had control in the native walled city, and the European troops were kept busy guarding the settlement from the depredations of the numerous roving bands of Boxers. The last armored train from Tientsin, carrying refugee women and children, got through to Tangku on the 16th. On the same day the Boxers made their first attack on the settlement and burned several houses before being driven off. They also attacked the railway station, which was held by the Russians. The following day they attacked several places on the railroad line, but all assaults were repulsed without loss to the allies.

The bombardment of the Taku forts seemed to be the signal for heavier attacks and increased activity by the Chinese. At 3 P.M. on June 17 the bombardment of Tientsin commenced, and shells began to fall in the foreign quarter. The military school on the river opposite the British concession was occupied by the Chinese, who had mounted some guns there. The school was so close to the settlement and threatened its safety to such an extent that the allies decided to attack it. The assault was completely successful. It was so unexpected that only slight resistance was encountered. One British officer was killed and 4 men were wounded. The building and guns were destroyed, but the position was later reoccupied by the Chinese until they were driven out by the relief force on June 23.

The bombardment of the settlement, however, continued all night and all the next day without intermission, though on subsequent days there were occasional lulls. The Chinese artillery fire was accompanied by attacks of Boxers and Imperial troops in great numbers at various points. The allied troops defending the railway station on the 18th and 19th were particularly hard pressed more than once. Tientsin was fighting for its life from June 17th to the 23rd, when the relief force pushed through to its rescue. On the 26th the number of European troops was augmented by the return of the Seymour combined party, and fears for the safety of the garrison were now allayed.

The hostile Chinese continued to occupy the native walled city and contiguous towns and villages. They then extended their lines in a semicircle from the northeast to the southwest, resting their right on the racecourse and their left on the Lutai Canal, threatening the European settlements from three sides. They also mounted guns at various points in the walled city along the railroad embankment northeast of the city. These guns caused considerable damage and were so well masked that the allies had great trouble locating them.

Although the increased strength of the allied garrison relieved the apprehension of immediate danger, the situation was still grave. The Chinese continued to threaten the settlements, and since they regarded the return of the Seymour Expedition as a defeat for the foreigners, the antiforeign feeling spread and emboldened the enemy in their attacks. Many of these came from the large arsenal about two miles east-northeast of the British concession, and the Russians who were on that side of the river were eager to capture it. Known as the Eastern Arsenal, it was the scene of the defeat of the American-Russian relieving column on June 22 and of a previous effort by the Russians to drive out the enemy.

After obtaining the cooperation of the Germans, British, and Americans, the Russians commenced to bombard the arsenal on the morning of June 27. The Russians and Germans were to make the main attack, while the British and Americans (600 men) were to act in support or reserve. However, the Americans went into action as soon as they arrived. They marched parallel to the left face of the arsenal under a flanking fire until they reached a point where they could turn and face the arsenal; then they advanced under a harassing shrapnel fire to within 250 yards. Bayonets were fixed and a charge was ordered that drove the Chinese out. The Russians and Germans were likewise successful in their attacks on the center and right face of the arsenal. The assault having been favorably concluded, the British and Americans withdrew, and the arsenal was destroyed.

The Russians lost 1 officer (a doctor) and 6 men killed, and 42 men wounded; the British, 7 killed and 21 wounded. The Russian commander, General Stossel, gave high praise to the conduct of the Germans in the fighting, commending their gallantry, discipline, and professional knowledge. The American contingent consisted of Second Lieutenant W.E. Jolly and 40 men of the Marine Corps, accompanied by Lieutenant A.E. Harding who went along as a volunteer. In the assault the marines charged over the parapet with a British company, and being first in this part of the fight, Lieutenant Harding captured an Imperial flag. All the men were part of Major Waller's party. They had marched 97 miles in five days, fighting all the way, and living on one meal a day for six days.

After the destruction of the arsenal, the shelling of the settlement ceased for a while, although sniper fire continued and caused a few casualties among the outlying pickets. Reinforcements continued to arrive, and the position of the allies was strengthened by the daily arrival of fresh troops. Eight hundred Japanese arrived on June 29, bringing the allied strength up to about 8,300, of which 1,200 were Japanese. On July 2 a detachment of French marines arrived 340 strong with 6 mountain guns. River communication between Tientsin and Taku was now open all the way, and the railroad could be used within 12 miles of the town.

The allies undertook no other active operations pending the arrival of further reinforcements until July 1, when a reconnaissance was made by a combined force of Americans, British, Russians, and Japanese, about 1,200 men, toward the native city. This operation developed some opposition from a number of small enemy parties, but they were easily driven out. On July 3 another reconnaissance undertaken by the Russians on the left side of the river resulted in driving the Chinese from a new position they had taken up to the east, threatening the railroad station. This time assistance was required from some Japanese troops and a British 12-pounder before success was achieved.

On June 28 the Chinese flooded a part of the countryside near the western quarter of the native city by cutting the canal. If the intention was to annoy or inconvenience the allies, it failed, as the section flooded was a small area near the native city.

At about 5 A.M. on July 4 the Chinese artillery opened fire from several guns mounted near the railway bridge over a canal. Later, large bodies of troops were observed moving beyond the Western Arsenal, but, on being shelled, they withdrew and kept out of range. About 4 P.M. a determined attack was made on the railroad station by large numbers of Chinese, but it was repulsed. It is reported that the allies were greatly aided in their defense by a timely severe thunderstorm and heavy rainfall, which dampened the ardor of the attacking force that was pressing the allies hard when the storm broke. July 5 was quiet except for an attack by the Russians on the Chinese guns to the north of their camp. During this assault the Russians succeeded in moving two locomotives and three trucks from the exposed station to the protection of their own camp.

On July 6 the Chinese commenced firing from some guns they had succeeded in planting and masking 1,000 yards from the station. The efforts of the allied guns to silence them resulted in a general bombardment. Two naval 12-pounders from the *Terrible* and two 9-pounder Krupp guns from the Taku forts had arrived on July 4.

These, with the 12-pounders already possessed by the allies, were mounted on the mud wall and replied to the enemy's fire. It was difficult to locate the Chinese guns, positioned among ruined houses where their flash could hardly be seen. The French and Japanese field batteries joined in the firing, and soon the guns in the Chinese fort were temporarily silenced. The French set fire to the viceroy's yamen, and the Japanese shelled the arsenal, thus preventing the guns mounted there from firing at the 12-pounders that were firing at the forts in the city.

An attempt was made by Major Bruce, commander of the First Chinese Regiment (English), to capture a small rapid-fire gun that had been pushed up to within short range of the settlement. The sortie was a failure. The party was driven back with a loss of 2 killed and 5 wounded, Major Bruce and Ensign Esdaile being among the wounded. The latter was severely wounded and died the next day.

Chinese artillery fire was resumed on July 7, and at noon the allies again bombarded the forts as before. A Japanese cavalry reconnaissance was made to the southwest toward the racecourse. It immediately drew heavy rifle fire from that direction, confirming the suspicion that the enemy was endeavoring to work around to the south from the native city, which would threaten the allies' communications. During the night the grandstand and buildings were set on fire and destroyed. The following day the allies arranged a combined operation to drive the enemy from his position in a village near the racecourse to capture the Western Arsenal.

The international force was composed of 1,000 Japanese, 850 British, 400 Russians, and 150 Americans. It moved out before daylight on July 9 through the Taku gate and turned to the right, or west. There the Japanese and British artillery soon engaged the enemy, while the Japanese cavalry came in contact with a body of Boxers whom they charged and dispersed, killing about 200. Meantime the infantry had captured some of the Chinese fortifications, including four small Krupp guns and a few rifles. The infantry continued to advance, driving the Chinese back toward the Western Arsenal (the Hai-Kwang-Sze, or Joss House Arsenal). By the time the allied force reached the arsenal from the south, another detachment of Japanese and Americans had arrived, having marched along Sankolins Wall from the settlement. The combined force assaulted the arsenal, which, after a short bombardment, was rushed and taken by the Americans and Japanese.

The Japanese then advanced beyond the arsenal toward the south wall of the city, but the Chinese had assembled there in force, and the heavy artillery and rifle fire made it inadvisable to proceed farther. Since the country to the west had been flooded by the enemy, it was impracticable to operate in that direction; so, after burning the arsenal, which was untenable by the allies, the expedition returned to its encampment. During the action the British and French concessions were heavily shelled by the Chinese from the northeastern batteries, but the damage was relatively insignificant.

The day's operations had been conducted by the Japanese, General Fukushima. The allied force was composed largely of Japanese troops who did most of the fighting. The mobility of their infantry and the dash and vigor of their cavalry were amply demonstrated during the conflict. Their casualties amounted to about 50 killed and wounded; the British had 1 killed and 3 wounded; the Russians and Americans had no casualties. The Chinese lost between 300 and 400 dead.

It was hoped that the success of the allies' attack would make the enemy withdraw into the walled native city. It did relieve the pressure on the allies' left by freeing the batteries in the British concession from the direct and enfilade fire that had been coming from the Western Arsenal, and by reducing the number of Chinese guns firing on the settlement. But the psychological effect on the enemy was not lasting, and they launched a very determined attack in force on the railroad. The situation had been held by the Russians from June 19 to July 4, when they withdrew. Subsequently the position was held in rotation by allied detachments. On July 11 the station was guarded by 100 men from each of the British, French, and Japanese contingents.

The attack on the Russian outposts by about 2,000 Chinese troops and Boxers commenced at 3 A.M. on the 11th. It was pushed so vigorously that many of the enemy got in between the tracks and the station. Half a Russian company was surrounded and had to fight its way out with fixed bayonets. The fighting lasted about three hours and was hotly waged on both sides. Eventually the enemy was driven off, with losses estimated between 350 to 500 killed. The allies had about 150 casualties, mostly among the French and Japanese. The Russian loss was 4 killed and 1 officer and 18 men wounded, and the British had 3 killed and 16 wounded. About noon the allies again bombarded the forts in the native city and succeeded in demolishing a pagoda near the fort in the city, which had been used as an observation post. The return fire, while heavy, was not damaging. In addition there were frequent attacks by small enemy parties, almost continuous sniper firing from nearby cover, and a daily shelling of the settlement at periodic intervals. The Chinese

The Capture of Tientsin 109

usually commenced before daylight, stopped before noon, and began again late in the afternoon.

One of the industries of Tientsin was the manufacture of coarse salt by the evaporation of sea water. The salt cakes were then stacked along the river bank and covered by matting, under which snipers concealed themselves. Since they used smokeless powder, they were hard to detect.

The most difficult positions the allies had to defend were the railway station and the French concession. The station was one of the main points of attack because the enemy desired to destroy the rolling stock and to secure an advantageous position from which to bombard the settlements. The French concession was the one nearest to the Chinese City and therefore suffered the most.

At this time the Russians occupied the Eastern Arsenal and had their own camp on the left bank of the Pei Ho south of the railway station. The other nationalities were located on the right bank of the river, mainly in their respective settlements, but varying their dispositions as required. All the allies responded promptly and willingly to calls for cooperation and assistance among themselves. The Germans were in the university grounds at the extreme southeast end of their concession. Their objective was to keep the Pei Ho open for communication with Taku, and this they successfully accomplished. There was no interruption in forwarding supplies to the full capacity of the lighters available.

On July 11 the strength of the allied forces in Tientsin was as follows: Russians, 4,450; Japanese, 3,090; French, 2,160; British, 1,420; Americans, 560; Germans, 400; Austrians, 50; and Italians, 40—making a grand total of 12,170. The strength of the enemy cannot be stated positively, but Admiral Seymour believed it was not fewer than 20,000, counting Boxers and regular Chinese soldiers. It included the troops of General Nieh's army that had originally pretended to oppose the Boxers, but soon took off the mask and openly opposed the allied troops in the Seymour Relief Expedition. This Chinese army contained about 13,000 men, some of whom had been drilled by German and Russian officers. They were well armed with Mauser rifles, equipped with artillery guns of mixed caliber and Maxims, but they were poorly disciplined. General Nieh was variously reported to have been killed in the allied attack on July 9 or to have committed suicide because of the Chinese reverses.

The Chinese army, threatening the allies and opposing their advance to save Peking, was superior in fighting qualities to any Orientals previously known to Europeans. In addition to the modern weapons and the training received from their foes, the Chinese were inspired by their hatred of foreigners and religious fanaticism to an intrepidity alien to their ordinary habits. This was demonstrated by their repeated fierce attacks and their stubborn resistance when they were attacked. They had ample supplies of all kinds of modern warfare stores, and the extent of their preparation was shown by the immense quantities that were found and destroyed by Admiral Seymour at Haiku and by the allies in the arsenal near Tientsin. These stores were valued at many millions of dollars.

The heavy artillery at the disposal of the allies was markedly inadequate and was considerably inferior to that of the Chinese—which seemed to be increasing in quantity daily and which they operated efficiently. Many of the allies believed that the positions of the allied troops were signaled or somehow made known to the Chinese by spies inside the lines, and that the Chinese must have had the assistance of Europeans in the operating of their guns. This last statement was made on the authority of skilled observers who claimed to have seen European technicians with Chinese gun crews.

The allies also labored under the disadvantage of being a polyglot army with varying systems of supply and drill, and without a single controlling head, or a definite plan of operations. In arranging movements or operations requiring the cooperation of several contingents, the various commanders had to exchange messages suggesting plans that might—or might not—be agreed upon.

So far they had been obliged to confine their operations to those necessary for holding their positions and keeping their communications intact. But the daily losses from the enemy's bombardment, and the opportune arrival of reinforcements of Japanese and Americans on July 11, hastened the adoption of plans to capture the city and drive the Chinese away.

Until the middle of June the United States had hoped to be able to do all that was necessary for the protection of the lives and property of its citizens in China by means of its naval forces. The situation had become so grave, however, that the dispatch of troops was decided reluctantly, and instructions were sent to the military commander in the Philippines to designate the organizations available for this service. The first of the units to receive movement orders was the Ninth Infantry. A severe storm that damaged the railroad and prevented the command from reaching Manila from field service in the provinces delayed its departure until June 27. The regiment sailed on the transports *Logan* and *Port Albert* with a strength of 39 officers and 1,271 men. It was commanded by Colonel E.H. Liscum, a veteran who had been severely wounded in both the Civil War and the Spanish-American War.

The Capture of Tientsin

Two battalions of the regiment that arrived at Taku on Saturday, July 7, were lightered ashore on the 10th and towed up the river the next day, reaching Tientsin in the evening. A few hours later a battalion of U.S. Marines, under Colonel Meade, who left Taku at 8 A.M., arrived. The third battalion of the Ninth arrived in Tientsin in time to participate in the fighting on July 13. The theory adopted by our Government, that the Chinese troubles were due to the excesses of irresponsible natives who could not be controlled by Chinese authorities, was expressed in Colonel Liscum's orders. He was directed to proceed to Peking via Taku and Tientsin, report to the American minister there, and cooperate with him in establishing order. General Fukushima, with a body of Japanese troops, arrived about the same time as the Ninth Infantry. Admiral Seymour, who had been the ranking senior officer, returned with his staff to his flagship off the Taku bar, and the officers and men of the *Centurion*, who had been with him on the relief expedition, were sent back to their ship.

The conduct of military operations was now assumed by General Fukushima as ranking officer of the allied forces present in Tientsin. The arrival of the Ninth Infantry and the U.S. Marines, together with a substantial reinforcement of Japanese troops, had so augmented the strength of the allied forces that on July 11 an attack on the whole Chinese position was projected, with the object of capturing the city and driving the enemy from all their strongholds. As finally arranged, the plan was that the Russians and Germans were to attack the enemy's position to the northeast of the city, while the Japanese, British, French, and Americans were to move from the southwest. For the latter movement it was decided that the allies would be in line at 3 A.M. and march in three columns, 500 yards apart, on the Western Arsenal; the French, 900 strong, on the right were to move to their position by crossing the mud wall in the British concession; the center column, consisting of 1,500 Japanese, to go by way of the racecourse gate; the left column, composed of six companies of the Ninth Infantry and a detachment of U.S. Marines (about 900 men in all), and the British contingent of 800 men (500 military, 300 naval) to proceed out the Taku gate. To the left of the left column was a body of about 150 Japanese cavalry.

The arsenal, which had been reoccupied by the Chinese after the operations on July 9, was recaptured by the Japanese, who were the first on the ground. The left column was delayed by the necessity of clearing out small parties of the enemy from the villages during its advance. The French were delayed at a bridge in the mud wall, which they had to cross while exposed to fire. The allies were now in position, however, along the mud wall. The Ninth Infantry and U.S. Marines, with the British, were west of the arsenal. The combined artillery units were located a short distance south of the wall and began to bombard the city about 5:30 A.M. After an hour's artillery fire, the allied attack was launched; the French on the right, the Japanese in the center, and the British and Americans on the left. The objective was the south gate.

The attack was begun by the Japanese, and their eagerness to advance necessitated a rapid movement, supported by heavy fire from the marines and English fusiliers, to get into position on the French left. The Ninth Infantry had been selected to support the attack of the left Japanese elements and marines and fusiliers. In the hurry and excitement of the occasion the order for this movement either was incorrectly given or was misunderstood by Colonel Liscum, who led the regiment to the right after passing through the gate in the mud wall. They immediately came under heavy destructive fire from the fort and wall and from a line of loopholed mud houses on their right front near the city wall. The regiment deployed hastily and advanced by a series of rushes, finally reaching the canal outside the city where they were compelled to halt, taking such cover as was available. While crossing one of the numerous dikes, the color bearer was hit. Colonel Liscum picked up the flag and, while apparently looking for a ford or some way of crossing, he was shot in the abdomen and fell, fatally wounded.

The regiment's position was a hazardous one. While somewhat sheltered from fire from the south wall, it was exposed to fire from hidden snipers. The distance from two Chinese guns across the canal was only about 75 yards, and there was also a deadly fusillade from the German flour mill about 300 yards to the right front, where the enemy was strongly intrenched. The U.S. consul, Mr. J.W. Ragsdale, who was present during part of the engagement, reported: "The shelling was far more terrific than any I experienced during the Civil War, and I served under General Sherman." By sunset the regiment had suffered heavy losses in killed and wounded. Colonel Liscum and 22 men were killed, and 3 officers and 70 men were wounded. It was reported that the dark blue shirts worn by the men of the Ninth offered a conspicuous target for the Chinese rifles.

The country around Tientsin to the west is described as a wasteland of marshes with lagoons and wandering rivers. The Chang Ho, the Hun Ho, and smaller streams join the Pei Ho somewhere in this marsh. To the north of the city were rice fields and gardens, and beyond these were the marshes. A railway, built on an embankment created by dirt fill between the two parallel rows of bamboo

The Capture of Tientsin 113

driven into the earth, crossed the marshland. To the south, however, where the marines crossed the wall in skirmish order, the country between the wall and the city was flat and level. There were great numbers of grave mounds, dikes, and ditches that were used as ready-made trenches. They were particularly advantageous on the open, fire-swept plain, since without them trenches would have had to be dug with bayonets.

During the day the Chinese kept up a terrific fire from machine guns and modern rifles as well as from jingals, one of their favorite weapons. These were an adaptation of the breech-loading action to a barrel about 7 feet long that required two and sometimes three men to fire. They had a long range, and when they hit, the bullets were heavy enough to stop almost anything. The wall of the native city was well manned with artillerymen of the Imperial army and Boxers. Many were armed with old-fashioned and obsolete weapons, muzzle-loaders and matchlocks. In the suburbs outside the south gate great numbers of Boxers sniped from concealment among the mud houses and grave mounds.

The plan for the attack included the cooperation of the naval guns under the direction of Captain Bayley of the Royal Navy. They were controlled by telephone from a signal tower in the British concession. They were ready to go into action at 4 A.M., but because of darkness and mist, firing was not commenced until a half hour later. A heavy fire was kept up to the west to drive enemy troops from the wall on both sides of the south gate as the allied troops advanced to the southwest, until signaled to cease firing, as the Japanese had entered the city. This message was sent by General Dorward in response to a request received from General Fukishima's chief of staff about 1 P.M. Shortly thereafter the allies started a general assault. The advancing troops, however, were met by such heavy fire from the wall, which increased in intensity as the troops moved forward, that it was apparent the Japanese had not entered the city. The assaulting troops were forced to take cover close to the canal around the city, and orders were sent for the guns to open fire again. The firing was so effective that the troops in the advanced trenches suffered few losses during the remainder of the day.

The U.S. Marines and the British fusiliers had reached an advanced position and occupied a line of trenches on the left, about 800 yards from the enemy. Directly in front of them was a bad swamp, through which a stream wandered aimlessly. Further advance in that direction was impossible. They were subjected to severe fire during the day, but they protected the left flank and repelled two enemy attempts to flank the allied troops, one about 8 A.M. and another about 2 P.M.

Toward evening the most threatening effort of the day was made on the same flank by large bodies of the enemy. With the assistance of the naval guns that concentrated their entire fire on the enemy, and under cover of rifle fire from troops on that flank, the attack was thrown back. After dark the marines and fusiliers were withdrawn with slight losses and regrouped behind the mud wall.

This withdrawal was most difficult, however, the enemy having the range so accurately that his shot struck the crest of the trenches and threw dirt in the faces of the men. The attack was made by small parties of eight or ten men by rushing from one mound or trench to another. The dead and wounded had been previously moved to the rear. General Dorward stated in his official report that the movement reflected great credit on the American commander, Colonel Meade, and Captain Gwynne of the fusiliers.

The Ninth Infantry was then extricated from its position after dark, covered by the fire of naval guns aimed at the barriers along the fringe of houses between the French settlement and the city, where most of the enemy fire was concentrated. With the assistance of an English naval detachment, the dead and wounded were brought back, and the regiment reached the mud wall in safety. Early in the attack two French companies had been detailed to clean out the Chinese from the ground between the French settlement and the city, from which later came the deadly fire on the Ninth Infantry. The French, however, were unable to make any progress and abandoned the effort.

The Japanese and other troops still clung to their advanced positions close to the city wall and, with their flanks and rear protected by other troops, they endeavored to make themselves as secure as possible. Provisions and water were sent forward to the troops on the line by the British commander. The day had been an unusually hot, trying one for the attacking force; but they cheerfully endured the hardships and bravely faced the dangerous fire for many hours. During the night a light rain fell. About 3 A.M. the next day, July 14, the Japanese sappers crossed the canal by a bridge they had constructed during the night. They blew in the outer gate and, after clambering over it, opened the inner gate. The Chinese had withdrawn during the night to the suburbs north and west, and the allied troops entered without opposition.

In a letter written to Marine Corps Colonel R.L. Meade immediately after the fight, General Dorward assumed the blame for the error of the Ninth Infantry's proceeding to the right instead of to the left and "for not remembering that troops wholly fresh to the scene of action and hurried forward in the excitement of attack were likely to lose their way," but he pointed out that the position taken up by the regiment and so gallantly maintained all day under a galling fire "undoubtedly prevented a large body of the enemy from turning the right of the attacking line and inflicting serious loss on the French and Japanese."

Colonel Meade reported the following casualties in the attack on the south gate:

> Americans: 24 killed, 98 wounded, 1 missing.
> English: 17 killed, 87 wounded.
> Japanese: 320 killed and wounded.
> French: 13 killed, 50 wounded.
> Russians and Germans: 140 killed and wounded.
> Total killed, wounded, and missing: 750.

The Russian column moved out on the other side of the river. It had been arranged that, having the longer march, they should move in time to attack the batteries at 10 A.M. The forces on the south were to attack as early as possible in order to attract the bulk of the Chinese to that side of the river and thus facilitate the capture of the batteries by the Russians. A German report of the operation states that the force consisted of twelve companies of Russian troops and two German troops, with two Russian field batteries and a French mountain gun battery; that by an eastward movement they outflanked and captured the Chinese northeast position north of the Lutai Canal and others along the railroad embankment east of the city, capturing 12 guns and blowing up 2 magazines. The report also states that the Russian general in his report named the Germans as capturing the guns and exploding the magazines and distinguishing themselves in the vanguard. Their casualties were 6 Germans wounded. The Russian column was commanded by General Stossel. The German contingent was composed of men from the *Gefion,* the *Irene,* and the *Kaiser Augusta,* commanded by Captain Weniger.

Other contemporary accounts mention only the explosion near the Lutai Canal. The weight of evidence seems to give the credit for the explosion of this magazine, which was full of brown powder, to a shell from the French battery. The blast occurred about 5 A.M. and was described as being of tremendous violence, throwing a column of black smoke 600 feet in the air and breaking glass and shaking buildings in the settlement. Luckily it caused no serious casualties among the allied forces only 500 to 600 yards away, although many horses and men were knocked off their feet, and the mules of the French battery bolted. General Stossel was thrown from his horse and received slight injuries from falling debris, but was able to resume his command after an hour's rest.

After the capture of the outlying Chinese positions, a movement in two columns, one a flanking operation from the right, was made against the fort near the city. But the stubborn resistance could not be overcome, and the allies succeeded only in holding the ground they had gained after driving the Chinese back on one side.

On July 14, after the allied entry into the city, the Northeast Fort was captured about noon with the assistance of the Japanese. Previous plans by the Russians to bring up additional artillery and repeat the attack were not implemented. The American troops, detachments of the Ninth Infantry and U.S. Marines, assisted in the operations on the north and east. Being located near the railroad station, which in itself was a dangerous position, they were exposed to severe fire from the Chinese artillery during the day and suffered heavy casualties.

After the city was taken, the allied forces pushed on as far as possible to the northern suburbs where they captured about 200 junks that afterwards proved very useful in the advance on Peking. A system of military government was soon instituted. The city of Tientsin was divided into four districts for administrative and police purposes, with each district under the control of one of the nationalities. The division of Berlin after World War II is somewhat reminiscent of Tientsin and Peking in 1900.

The suburbs of the city gave an indication of the conditions inside the city. When the allies fought their way to the walls they saw dozens of headless bodies with the hands tied behind their backs floating in the canals and ditches. Rows of heads, hung by their pigtails, decorated the outer wall—all beheaded by their own people either because they refused to fight or were suspected of being in sympathy with the foreigners. As described by various correspondents, the conditions existing inside the walled city when the allies entered further exemplified in a most striking manner the horrors of war. Hundreds of Chinese dead lay about in the streets or were piled along ths walls; the wounded lay as if dead when approached, fearing to be killed—as doubtless many were. The stench arising from dead animals was intolerable. The overheated air was sodden with smoke and the noisome smell of carrion. Swollen corpses were strewn about in every position of agony; swarms of flies clustered on the bodies, arising with an angry buzz when disturbed. Everywhere there was evidence of the immense damage done by the allied guns. Among the smoldering ruins of shattered and burning houses, charred corpses were being eaten by starving pigs and dogs.

The Capture of Tientsin

The city wall itself sustained little damage notwithstanding the tremendous volume of allied artillery fire aimed at it.

Under normal conditions the city festered with the accumulated rubbish from a dense population packed into a labyrinth of hovels around the palaces of viceroys and petty officials. There was no exaggeration in the words of one writer who said that "the walls of the city, on the day it was occupied, surrounded a square mile of such filth, ruin, and death, such turmoil and pillage as history could hardly duplicate." The looting and pillage of the city, done mostly by the natives, but joined in by many Europeans, was entirely unrestrained on the first day. Later, as soon as they could give it their attention, the allied commanders adopted severe repressive measures to put a stop to it, and the scandal was soon discontinued. The Japanese, because of the admirable discipline that prevailed in their units, are said to have done the least looting. Strict orders from U.S. officers and the training and discipline of U.S. troops mostly prevented American service personnel from participating in the orgy of thievery and looting.

The occupational duties of the allies included reestablishing order, carrying out absolutely essential sanitary measures, providing for the care of the sick and wounded, and the supply and welfare of their troops. There were also certain military problems to be handled, which included guarding against attack, securing their lines of communication, performing frequent reconnaissance to keep informed of the enemy's forces and their locations, and preparing for the advance on Peking to relieve the beseiged legations. The allied commanders and their troops had ample duties to keep them fully occupied.

Chapter VIII

The Peking Relief Expedition Takes Shape

The situation at Peking, temporarily obscured by affairs at Tientsin, again became the subject of deepest interest. The intense anxiety of the civilized world for the safety of the foreigners and the desire for their rescue created great impatience at the seemingly unnecessary delay in beginning the relief expedition, and considerable criticism of the allied commanders appeared in the daily press.

As usual the estimates of the Chinese forces were widely divergent and ranged from 8,000 to 30,000 troops who might oppose the allied march to Peking. This disparity was not surprising, since even in peacetime no one knew the real strength of the Chinese army, not even the Chinese government itself. Even if it were known, it would be merely a statement of the number of men it contained officially and would be of no real value because many of those enrolled were neither armed nor equipped, and others were not performing military service but were pursuing civilian vocations.

The allied commanders held frequent conferences and agreed generally that an advance was impracticable without substantial reinforcements and additional supplies of all kinds. These were continually arriving, and the task of preparing for the advance kept all personnel diligently occupied with their assigned duties. The obstinate and stubborn resistance of the Chinese in the fighting that had already taken place showed that their armies had profited by foreign military instruction and indicated the grave consequences should a reverse occur to the relief expedition. Once started, the expedition must be strong enough to overcome any opposition it might encounter.

The reports received from Peking about this time were conflicting. Circumstantial accounts of the massacre of the Europeans in Peking on July 6 and 7, published on July 16 by what was subsequently called the "Shanghai Liar," came as a shock to the civilized world,

The Peking Relief Expedition Takes Shape 119

and in Europe the report of the massacre of foreigners was gradually but reluctantly accepted as being true. This belief may have dulled the urgency of the preparations for the rescue, since if there were no foreigners left to save, there was no need to hurry. In America, however, the following message from Mr. Conger, dated July 16, was received in Washington on July 20:

> For one month we have been besieged in British legation under continued shot and shell from Chinese troops. Quick relief only can prevent general massacre.

This message, which showed that at least some foreigners were still alive on July 16, was fully accepted by the U.S. Government, which urged the earliest possible start of the relief expedition and impressed these views on the American commanders in China.

From the outset of the dangerous Boxer uprising, interested powers had sent troops and war vessels to China. On June 30 British Admiral Bruce reported the forces landed as of that date to be:

Country	Officers	Men
Russia	117	5,817
Japan	119	3,709
Great Britain	184	1,700
Germany	44	1,300
France	17	387
United States	20	329
Italy	7	131
Austria	12	127
Total	520	13,500

The arms included 53 field guns and 36 machine guns.

Reinforcements were arriving daily, and 10 days later it was estimated that the force at the disposal of the powers was about 20,000. On July 11 the London *Times* published a statement of the naval strength of the powers in Chinese waters. It reported that England had 2 battleships, 3 armored cruisers, 2 protected cruisers of the first class and 3 of the second class, 1 dispatch vessel, 4 sloops, 2 gunboats, and 4 torpedo-boat destroyers, all having a complement of 6,000. Also en route or under orders to proceed there were 2 battleships; 1 first-, 3 second-, and 2 third-class protected cruisers; and 2 gunboats—having a total complement of 4,000.

The British forces landed included, besides seamen and marines from the various ships, 384 officers and men of the Second Royal Welsh Fusiliers and Royal Engineers; 4 companies of the Hong Kong Regiment, which was recruited from Mohammedans of the Punjab; 1 mountain and 1 field battery of the Asiatic Artillery, all from Hong Kong; and 200 men of the Chinese regiment from Weihaiwei. The Indian contingent, then embarking for China under the command of Lieutenant General Sir Alfred Gaselee, consisted of 223 British officers, 308 British warrant and noncommissioned officers, and 9,540 native officers and men, with 7,170 camp followers, 1,280 horses and ponies, 2,060 mules, 6 guns and 11 Maxims.

The Russian naval force consisted of 3 battleships, 3 armored cruisers, 1 protected cruiser of the second class, and 2 armored gun vessels, with a complement of 4,500; besides 1 armored cruiser on the way with a strength of 567. Other vessels were on the station or on the way from Vladivostok; and at either Port Arthur or Taku there were 7 torpedo gunboats, having a complement of about 800. The Russian troops landed at Taku up to the middle of June totaled 3,000 and were commanded by General Stossel. This number was nearly doubled by the end of the month, and it was believed that more had since been landed, mainly drawn from the garrison at Port Arthur.

The Germans had 1 first- and 4 second-class protected cruisers and 3 gunboats, with a complement of 2,219; and under orders on the way, 6 battleships, 1 armored cruiser, 1 third-class protected cruiser, and 1 dispatch vessel, totaling 4,600 men. They had already landed 1,350 officers and men from the ships, including some troops from the garrison at Kiaochow comprising a field battery, a Chinese company, a pioneer section, some naval artillery and marines. There were 2,300 marines under command of General von Hoepner en route and a battery of 3.4-inch guns and 1,200 men to become relief crews for the ships that were arriving. The German forces proposed for China were to consist of a corps of more than 10,000 men, principally infantry. Two battalions of 800 men each were to be taken from infantry regiments in Germany, and about 1,100 cavalry troops were to arrive. For economy the horses were to be purchased in the Dutch colonies and transported on steamers of the North German Lloyd Company.

The German artillery was to consist of 2 field batteries and 1 mortar battery. Since there were 3 field batteries already at Kiaochow, the troops had 36 field guns at their disposal. Large units of pioneers and detachments of railway troops were also to be sent in the belief that conditions would make their services very necessary. With the 3,300 troops already arrived or en route, the total German

The Peking Relief Expedition Takes Shape 121

strength would exceed 15,000 men. Moreover, the Kaiser had ordered further reinforcements consisting of 1 infantry brigade of 8 battalions on a war footing, 3 squadrons of cavalry, 4 batteries and 1 field howitzer—all of which were to be comprised of volunteers from the active army—and they were to leave at the end of July.

On July 26 Berlin advised that in addition to the regular forces (naval and marine infantry) already departed or soon to leave for China, the government had organized an East Asiatic expeditionary corps under the command of Lieutenant General von Lessel. It was to consist of 2 brigades of infantry, of 2 regiments having 8 companies each and commanded by major generals; 1 cavalry regiment of 3 squadrons; 1 field artillery regiment of 4 batteries; various howitzer batteries, ammunition, and train detachments; and the necessary staff. The advanced detachment of this corps sailed from Genoa on July 24. A large part was to leave from Bremerhaven on the 28th, and the remainder about a week later.

The French naval force comprised 1 first-class and 3 second-class protected cruisers and 2 gunboats, having a total complement of 1,800. On the way and under orders were 1 armored cruiser, 1 first-class and 5 second-class protected cruisers, with a total strength of 2,300. A force of about 400 French bluejackets had been landed up to June 30 from the French ships commanded by Rear Admiral Courrejolles. Marine troops were also sent from Saigon, and 2,000 were expected to have arrived by July 3. On June 29, a force of 2,500 left Toulon, and 3 battalions of infantry, 2 batteries of artillery with 75 horses and mules, sections of telegraphists and hospital attendants, and stores, supplies, and ammunition were shipped out early in July. Another battalion of marines was being organized there, and a brigadier general was expected to proceed to Taku to take command of the forces.

As of July 26 the French expeditionary forces for service in China was to be a division of the following composition:

First Brigade, General Frey commanding.
   3 regiments of marine infantry (16th, 17th and 18th), 5,400 men.
   4 mountain batteries and 2 field batteries, with 3.15-inch guns, 800 men, and 720 mules.
   Artillery mechanics, engineers, hospital corpsmen, etc.

Second Brigade, General Bailloud commanding.
   1 regiment of Zouaves, 4,000 men.
   1 regiment of infantry, 3,000 men.

3 batteries of 3-inch guns, 550 men and 95 mules.
2 squadrons of Chasseurs d'Afrique, 300 men and 300 horses.

In addition there were 3 detachments: park artillery, divisional engineers, and general service personnel. The total force was expected to have a strength of 15,220 men.

Of those listed above, the Sixteenth Marine Infantry, 2 mountain batteries, and 1 field battery were already at Taku. Except for 1 battery, the remainder of the first brigade sailed from Toulon about August 1. The second brigade was to sail from France and Algeria between the 10th and 20th. France was also considering the advisability of sending a battery of 4.7-inch guns, two companies of troops of the train, a section of railroad troops, and a balloon section. A number of coolies for service with the troops (10 for each company or battery) were to be sent from Saigon.

The Italians had 2 third-class protected cruisers at Taku with 514 men, and 2 armored cruisers and 2 second-class protected cruisers on the way with a complement of 1,550. Seven officers and 131 men had been landed, and an expeditionary corps of 2,000 men—half infantry of the ilne and half bersaglieri—were to sail from Italy about July 15.

Austria had 1 torpedo cruiser on the station, the *Zenta*, from which 140 officers and men had been sent ashore. This force was to be augmented by the addition of 2 armored cruisers and 1 second-class protected cruiser with a complement of 1,350.

The Japanese naval force comprised 1 armored cruiser, 4 second-class and 3 third-class protected cruisers, with a complement of 2,740, besides several torpedo destroyers. A battleship, an armored cruiser, and a second-class protected cruiser were known to be under orders, and other formidable vessels were available if required. By June 30 more than 3,800 Japanese troops had been landed, and additional forces were being rapidly moved to China.

On July 11 the United States had in China the battleship *Oregon*, the cruisers *Baltimore, Newark, Don Juan de Austria,* and the gunboats *Helena, Nashville, Yorktown,* and *Monocacy.* The *Oregon* left Hong Kong for Taku on June 24, but was severely damaged when it hit an uncharted rock, and had to undergo repairs at the Japanese government docks at Kuri. The *Brooklyn* had arrived a few days before from Manila with Admiral Remey, who was to succeed Admiral Kempff, on board. The cruiser *Buffalo* and the *Iris, Alexander, Saturn,* and *Hannibal* were under orders for Taku, and the gunboats *Princeton* and *Marietta* were ordered to be in readiness.

By June, Admiral Kempff had landed 20 officers and 329 men,

The Peking Relief Expedition Takes Shape

with guns, from the ships at Taku. The Ninth Infantry and a battalion of marines had reached Tientsin on July 11 in time to participate in the attack on the walled city on the 13th.

The Fourteenth Infantry, commanded by Colonel A.S. Daggett, and Captain Henry J. Reilly's Battery F of the Fifth Artillery sailed from Manila on July 15 on the transports *Indiana* and *Flintshire*. They were already at Tientsin when Major General Adna R. Chaffee arrived at Taku on the *Grant* about the end of July. Also on the *Grant* were the Sixth Cavalry and a number of unassigned recruits for the organizations already on shore. These were disembarked as expeditiously as possible, but the lack of facilities presented some unloading problems. It will be told in a subsequent chapter how it took two days to off-load the horses for Reilly's Battery.

There were now landed:

Organization	Officers	Men	Total
Sixth Cavalry and recruits	27	1,083	1,110
Battery F, Fifth Artillery	4	138	142
Ninth Infantry, 12 companies	39	1,271	1,310
Fourteenth Infantry, 8 companies	26	1,118	1,144
Total	96	3,610	3,706

Ordered to Nagasaki and available for service in China, if required:

Organization	Officers	Men	Total
E, Engineer Battalion	2	150	152
First Cavalry, 8 troops	20	834	854
Third Cavalry, 4 troops	10	428	438
Ninth Cavalry, 8 troops	20	834	854
Third Artillery, 4 batteries	11	452	463
Seventh Artillery, 3 batteries	9	469	478
First Infantry, 8 companies	24	1,058	1,082
Second Infantry, 8 companies	22	1,058	1,080
Fifth Infantry, 8 companies	22	1,058	1,080
Eighth Infantry, 8 companies	22	1,058	1,080
Fifteenth Infantry, 8 companies	22	1,058	1,080
Total	184	8,457	8,641

In addition to those listed above, the Third and Seventeenth Infantry regiments were ordered to be in readiness, and 500 marines were then on the way to China, which with those already in China would make 3 battalions of 400 men each.

The Secretary of War's directive designating Major General Adna R. Chaffee as the commander of U.S. troops in China is contained in the following message:

> Adjutant-General's Office
> Washington, July 19, 1900.
>
> General CHAFFEE:
> (Care Hyde, Nagasaki.)
>
> Secretary War directs that you proceed at once with transport *Grant*, Sixth Cavalry, and marines to Taku, China, and take command of American land forces, which will be an independent command known as the China relief expedition. You will find there the Ninth and Fourteenth Infantry, one battery of the Fifth Artillery, and one battalion of marines. . . . Reinforcements will follow to make your force in the immediate future up to 5,000, and very soon to 10,000. . . . Under one hundred and twenty-second article of war your command will include marines on shore. Confer freely with admiral in command of fleet. Complete understanding and cooperation between the two services is enjoined by the President, and message to that effect has been sent admiral in command naval force. Reports now indicate that American minister with all the legation have been destroyed in Pekin. Chinese representative, however, insists to the contrary, and there is, therefore, a hope which you will not lose sight of until certainty is absolute. It is the desire of this Government to maintain its relations of friendship with the part of Chinese people and Chinese officials not concerned in outrages on Americans. Among these we consider Li Hung Chang, just appointed Viceroy of Chihli. You will to the extent of your power aid the Government of China or any part thereof in repressing such outrages and in rescuing Americans, and in protecting American citizens and interests, and wherever Chinese Government fails to render such protection you will do all in your power to supply it. Confer freely with commanders of other national forces, act concurrently with them, and seek harmony of action along the lines of similar purpose and interest. There should be full and free conference as to operations before they are entered upon. You are at liberty to agree with them from time to time as to a common official direction of the various forces in their combined operations, preserving, however, the integrity of your own American division, ready to be used as a separate and complete organization. Much must be left to your wise discretion and that of the admiral. . . . The President has to-day appointed you major-general of volunteers. . . .
>
> Corbin

Careful preparations were made by the various staff departments of the U.S. Army for the equipment and supply of the troops and the care of the sick and wounded. By July 17 the following actions had been taken by each department:

Medical Department

The troops from Manila had with them 8 medical officers, 46 hospital corpsmen, regimental field hospitals of 25 beds, and equipment for a 350-bed general hospital; medical supplies for 5,000 men for three months, and a hospital fund of $500.

A total of 18 medical officers had already sailed from San Francisco, one of whom was provided with $50,000 of public funds from the medical and hospital appropriation and $1,000 from hospital funds. In addition 78 assigned and unassigned members of the hospital corps had also sailed. The *Meade* was scheduled to sail from San Francisco on August 1 with 8 or more medical officers, one of whom was Assistant Surgeon Fuller, U.S.A. He was assigned to the Fifteenth Infantry and was to have a 50-bed field hospital. He also carried $10,000 of hospital funds. Eighteen hospital corpsmen were also to sail on the *Meade*.

Subsistence Department

The chief commissary officer at Manila, who was charged with the supply of troops in China, was furnished the information that enabled him to estimate and call for the necessary supplies, which were then ordered. Anticipating the future, the department had directed him to provide for the probable necessity of supplying the marines and seamen on shore service with the Army, and of having on hand at least six months' supply in the depot in China before November 1, when the usual obstruction to navigation by ice in the Gulf of Pechili might be expected. Fifty thousand dollars in gold had been invoiced to him for use in China.

The Ninth Infantry left Manila with 30 days' rations, and their transport carried to Taku a 3-months' supply for 5,000 men. The two squadrons of the Sixth Cavalry carried 85 days' field rations and three bake ovens. The Fifteenth Infantry was to take 60 days' field rations, which was the number supplied to all the troops then under orders, at the request of the commissary officer in Manila.

The meat ration furnished consisted of 40 days' bacon and 20 days' ration of canned meats—meat stew, corned beef hash, and corned beef. Fresh or dehydrated potatoes, or a combination of the two, were to be supplied from San Francisco. The chief commissary officers in Manila and China were informed as to the character of the meat ration for use in China and given all available information as to the possibility of procuring fresh meat and vegetables there. Manila was recommended as the most convenient point for the location of the main base of supply, with a secondary base to be located somewhere in China, probably at Taku.

Signal Corps

One first lieutenant and 10 men of the Signal Corps sailed with the Ninth Infantry, carrying material and instruments for 50 miles of field telegraph line. Two officers and 8 men with material for 100 miles of line sailed on the *Grant* with General Chaffee. Major George P. Scriven, signal officer of Volunteers, was ordered to report to General Chaffee as signal officer of the command. Four other Volunteer signal officers were available for foreign service if required.

Quartermaster's Department

Abundant supplies of winter clothing for the troops, including ponchos, arctic overshoes, and blanket-lined canvas hoods, and 1,400 Sibley stoves with 7,000 stovepipe joints were to be shipped from San Francisco on the transports departing on July 14 and August 1. Troops leaving the United States for China carried a complete outfit of tropical clothing in addition to their regulation winter clothing and tentage. Troops coming from the Philippines were fully equipped with tentage and a supply of unlined blouses, lightweight trousers, woolen undershirts, and cotton stockings and drawers. Dark blue flannel shirts sufficient for 5,000 men and 360 Sibley stoves were also shipped from Manila.

The Ninth Infantry was accompanied by 98 mules, 19 escort wagons, 4 ambulances, one Daugherty wagon (4-mule), one delivery wagon (2-mule), and forage for 30 days. The troops also carried ample supplies of all quartermaster's stores, and the regimental quartermasters were provided with funds for necessary local purchases.

The transports *Leelanaw* and *Connemaugh* from San Francisco and the *Lennox* from Portland carried the Sixth Cavalry's 901 horses, 14 draft and 100 pack mules, 28 riding horses for packers, and 2 bell mares; 100 aparejos (packsaddles) with the complement of packers, cargodores, etc., for two complete pack trains, and full supplies for 3 months of horse and mule shoes, nails, farriers' tools, veterinary medicines, rope, lanterns, etc. The pack trains, mules, and supplies were shipped on the *Lennox,* and the forage on the three vessels included oats for 196 days and hay for 98 days for all the animals. The quartermasters on the several transports had each been provided with $10,000 in gold from public funds. There was also ordered to be placed on the transport at San Francisco, on which the Fifteenth Infantry was to sail, a supply of paulins, stable

The Peking Relief Expedition Takes Shape

brooms, rakes, rope, nails, boilers for boiling drinking water, lanterns, buckets, water kegs, field cooking ranges, and carpenter tools for each company.

Four hundred thoroughly broken-in mules were en route to Seattle, available for use wherever needed, and 285 aparejos, 100 sterilizers having a capacity of 25 gallons per hour were being made to be sent to San Francisco by express as soon as possible. Eight were to be ready to go on the *Meade* on August 1, with two distilling plants having a capacity of 600 gallons a day. The sterilizers were intended to make river or other impure fresh water potable; and the distilling plants, besides performing that function, could also provide potable water from sea water. Additional distilling plants were to be shipped on succeeding transports until a sufficient number were furnished to meet the needs of 6,000 men.

Other items were attended to, such as the procuring and supply of lumber, fuel, and small cast-iron stoves that were obtainable in Japan and were suitable for the soft coal of that country. They were to be used by the troops to supplement the Sibley stoves. Arrangements were made for the transfer of troops and freight on Manila-bound transports sailing from San Francisco to lighter draft transports at Nagasaki for onward movement to Taku. Animal ships were chartered and fitted up as fast as they arrived to carry 4,000 animals, mules and horses, as they might be needed.

Ordnance Department

All ordnance supplies shipped from the United States but not going direct to China were to be sent to the base established at Manila—the Cavite Arsenal—unless a depot should be established at Nagasaki by courtesy of Japan. The Chief of Ordnance reported that there was readily available an abundant supply of ammunition for small arms and machine guns of rifle caliber for a prolonged war on a large scale. There were on hand 400 to 500 rounds for each of the large-caliber guns, and orders had already been placed for more. For all the service 3.2-inch field guns 500 rounds were on hand and provision had been made to keep up the supply indefinitely; all were of smokeless powder. There was an adequate supply of caliber-.45 black-powder cartridges that could be used for Gatling guns. The smokeless powder cartridges of that size that had been made for the Springfield rifle had proved unreliable in the Gatling guns.

In addition, orders had already been placed for 50 Colt automatic machine guns, caliber .30, complete with ammunition and accessories;

for 2 complete batteries, each having six 12-pounder Vickers-Maxim mountain guns and 300 rounds of ammunition; and for 2 batteries, each having six 1-pounders Vickers-Maxim automatic guns with 1,000 rounds of ammunition—all to be delivered at the earliest possible moment. The Navy authorized that 12 of the 25 guns being manufactured for it at the Colt factory be delivered to the Army, but they had to be sighted for ranges over 1,000 yards, which would take some time to accomplish.

The determination of the date for the advance was left by the powers to the several commanders, whose views doubtless differed and changed from time to time as circumstances altered. The commanders were also to determine the number of men required and the degree of preparation necessary. By July 23 the railroad from Taku to Tientsin had been reopened for traffic, and the number of allied troops in Tientsin was reported to be 28,000. By the end of the month their strength was increased by further arrivals of American, English, and Japanese reinforcements, including General Chaffee and Sir Alfred Gaselee, the commanders of the American and English forces.

From the tone of the press dispatches received about this time in the United States, it was feared that no advance could be made before the middle of August. It would seem to be a sufficient answer to the harsh criticisms that were leveled at the commanders that the advance was begun nearly two weeks earlier than expected. The discretion with which their plans were made was shown by the fact that the movement had been in progress for a day or so before it became known to the general public. The credit for the early start was mainly due to the American, English, and Japanese commanders who, following the instructions and wishes of their governments, collectively urged and finally impressed upon the others the absolute necessity for pressing forward to Peking at the earliest moment.

Nationality	Men	Guns
Japanese	10,000	24
Russians	4,000	16
British	3,000	12
Americans	2,000	6
French	800	12
Germans	200	0
Austrians and Italians	100	0
Total	20,100	70

The Peking Relief Expedition Takes Shape 129

At a meeting held on August 3 it was arranged to begin the advance on the following day with approximately 20,000 men. The composition of the relief expedition as it moved out on the afternoon of August 4 was as indicated on page 128.

The large buildup of forces programmed for action in China by several nations never materialized.

Chapter IX

Supply and Transport on the March

When the start was made from Tientsin on August 4, the sight presented by the enormous amount of road transportation is said to have beggared description. It included pack animals of all kinds—horses, ponies, mules, donkeys, camels—and carts of all sizes and shapes, from the little "coster's barrow" drawn by the Japanese ponies to what were called "the huge American prairie wagons, each drawn by four enormous mules," that trailed for miles behind the troops. Everything on wheels had been impressed into the transport service: Even the cows were bearing packs for the Japanese, and loaded camels plodded along with the Russian trains. Coolies dragged carts, staggered under heavy burdens, and poled or tugged up the river the clumsy junks or scows loaded with stores. Notwithstanding the seeming immensity of the trains, each contingent was hampered by the inadequacy of the means for moving its most necessary supplies.

Though American food and other supplies were infinitely more generous in quantity and quality than those of the other allies, they were not packed with scrupulous care for safe carriage and quick handling. In this respect the Japanese and British especially were without rivals. The Japanese allowed few packages to exceed 100 pounds in weight or 3 cubic feet in volume. All boxes generally, except ammunition cases, etc., were covered with rice straw, neatly sewed at the corners and tied in two directions with rope or braid of the straw. Sacks also were protected with the same outer covering. This material was light, strong, and very elastic and protected the inner case or sack so thoroughly that the loss from broken packages was negligible.

The smallness and moderate weight of the packages permitted rapid handling. Whether it was at a transport's side—12 miles off shore in a heavy swell—unloaded from lighters to wharfs, railroad

Supply and Transport on the March 131

at Tangku or Tientsin, or from the little river junks to store-piles, wagons, or pack trains at Tungchow, it aroused the envy of the American quartermaster officers to see the rapidity with which these homogeneous packages were handled. They fitted the coolie laborer and the coolie fitted them, for everything was actually carried on the head and shoulders. Contrast this with a case of stationery weighing 600 pounds put in a thin, flimsy white pine case, which, from rough handling and its own weakness, broke in pieces in the bottom of the junk. Imagine the time and supplies lost in repacking, for the coolie never failed to steal, even though he knew that a bamboo beating and the loss of his prized queue would be the inevitable result of being caught.

The British Indian Army practice was very much the same—small uniform packages with a heavy jute packing instead of the Japanese rice straw matting. One hundred and sixty pounds was the load for their pack mules, so their packages averaged about 80 pounds each, since their supplies were practically all transported by pack trains.

The Russians did not appear to have much in the way of supplies except for ammunition, which they had in large quantities. As with most of the allies, their supplies were packed in small, neat, strong packages of about 80 pounds.

The French Marine Infantry, who came from Tonkin, had a miscellaneous collection of stores of all shapes and sizes, evidently purchased for the occasion in various East Asian ports, judging from the markings on them. The French troops who came later had regular supplies, generally well packed but not with the same care as those of the British and Japanese. They also had some difficult packages to transport, viz: claret casks of great size and weight. It was a common occurrence for the monotony of the American teamsters' life to be broken by the sight of an obstinate Chinese mule, an irate Frenchman, and an overturned Peking cart with its load of a wine cask at the bottom of some gulley. The Italians and Austrians were often in a similar plight.

The German packing of their supplies was about as badly done as the American. Their stores were packed in flimsy boxes also, and at every shipping point were piles of broken cases. They had little or no transportation except what they had slowly collected in the country, and they experienced considerable difficulty trying to make a 4-foot box fit into a 3-foot cart.

American subsistence supplies, however, were well packed in strong cases of moderate weight and volume. Sacks were double-sacked and were quite strong. On the other hand American quartermaster supplies as a rule were very poorly packaged, the cases being too large and much too heavy. There was a greater proportion of breakage of cases in this class than in any other. It would also have been better to make the cases a size to fit the mule-drawn escort wagons. This same difficulty arose in handling ordnance stores, also put up in very bulky and heavy packages. For example, some cases of powder weighed 400 pounds net, and it took all the coolies who could crowd around it to lift such a case into a wagon. A 100-pound case would have been infinitely more practical. Medical supplies were better packed as regards weight and volume, but they were put in fragile cases that were much too weak to withstand the hard usage of the long and complex transportation.

None of the allied troops were as excellently or abundantly supplied with food as the Americans. One of the British officers inquired: "How often do your men get this excellent bacon?" The reply was, "Twenty-one times a week if they want it," which astounded the Englishman. The British white troops had a ration similar to the Americans in quality and quantity but not as varied or flexible, and they used tea instead of coffee. The British Indian troops had about ¾ of a pound of atta or flour, about 1 pound of rice, 1 gill of ghee or vegetable oil, salt, and once a week a pound of fresh meat, bone and all. The Sikhs used only mutton or goat, but the Mohammedans ate everything except pork.

The Japanese had rice, bread, dried fish, and tea, which they supplemented with sheep and cattle raised in the country. They also had American canned meats that were not used regularly but were more of a special or emergency diet.

The Russians had little besides black bread and soup. They were issued ¼-pound cans of some kind of meat preparation at intervals, much in the same manner as the Japanese used American meats. They had the finest cooking arrangement in the expedition. An iron furnace under a semi-spherical water-jacketed boiler was mounted on a springless carriage. The boiler was fitted with a tight cover, and the entire assembly was strongly and compactly built. Into this they put all the materials they had for a soup or stew, screwed down the cover, lighted the fire, and away went this perambulating soup tureen with its company. When camp was made all the men had to do was "Stack Arms," and then file past the soup machine. The cook opened a faucet and each man received his ration of hot, thick, well-cooked soup. In the meantime the assistant cook chopped up loaves of black bread with an ax and gave each man a liberal chunk. Americans who had tasted the bread several times reported that it did not improve on acquaintance, and that it seemed to have been made of equal parts of bran, sand, and sawdust, and besides, it was sour. Nevertheless the Russian method was an ideal and economical way to prepare a soldier's meal, but it is extremely doubtful that a steady diet of soup three times a day would be kindly viewed by American soldiers, although the Russians looked strong and healthy, and apparently thrived on it.

The Americans kept the best-policed (tidiest) and cleanest camps, all garbage being meticulously removed and buried in pits at some distance. Latrines were invariably established promptly and limed or covered with dry earth daily. In fact, there was no fault to be found with sanitary measures. It was second nature for the regular soldier to be clean and see to it that others were the same. Certainly they made life a burden to the Chinese by insisting that "John" clean out his streets and houses, which, judging from their condition at the time, had not been done since the visit of Marco Polo.

In such a cosmopolitan force it was only normal that likes and dislikes among the factions of the various nations should develop. All official relations of course were cordial and diplomatically correct, but this type of intercourse does not always reveal the real feelings of the individuals. The actual feelings became apparent in the association, or lack of it, among the various forces. For example, the Japanese was smiling and polite to all and in evidence in all the camps, especially the British and American. The Russian stayed to himself and did not even seem to care for his friend the Frenchman. The British and American troops were always together and constantly in each other's camps. The German also kept to himself as did the Frenchman, except when he was in the Russian camp. Undoubtedly, language barriers had some part in this.

In the matter of transportation none of the allies could touch the Americans. The amount was limited in the beginning but soon increased. Although the transport consisted only of escort wagons, their size and the amount they hauled amazed the foreigners. When they were told that these were our light wagons, sent because of the anticipated difficulty of Chinese roads, and that at home we habitually used a much larger, stronger wagon hauled by six mules and driven by one man with a single line, they listened politely but skeptically. Although the light wagons gave splendid service and held up well under heavy loads over rough roads, spare parts were not interchangeable on all wagons. There were three kinds of escort wagons and they all differed slightly. Obviously it would have been preferable to have all the wagons built to standard specifications where spare parts would be interchangeable, a prime necessity in a campaign.

The American wagons normally carried 3,500 to 4,000 pounds, according to the condition of the road. But even on the days when the other nations stopped their supply trains because of the mud, the Americans went through on schedule. Under the U.S. system one man cared for four mules, and each mule hauled from 700 to 1,000 pounds of stores. With the cart systems of other allies, this load never exceeded 500 pounds per animal, and each animal required one man to care for him. The American pack train also greatly surprised the foreigners. The system of putting the loads on so that they stayed there until unlashed was something new; the "diamond hitch" was indeed a mystery to them. Then, too, the speed at which they traveled and the small number of men required to pack and drive the train was equally astounding; but the one thing that caused the most comment was the manner in which the mules followed the bell mare. How 50 mules could be turned loose and kept under control, especially on herd, by a couple of men was remarkable, but when it came to driving them along a crowded road and through the labyrinthine streets of a Chinese city without decreasing the speed, losing a mule, or stopping to adjust loads, the others simply marveled.

The Japanese had a number of pack horses, fierce little Japanese stallions with shaggy manes and bulging eyes, that were led by soldiers. Horse and man were generally executing a sort of waltz in the dust, and they were not very satisfactory. Principal dependence was on small one-horse carts consisting of a light platform and shafts mounted on two small wheels. They had neither sides nor ends and, though of light construction, were strong. Their maximum load was about 500 pounds, and each horse was led by a soldier. The carts and horses were well handled and efficient, although not as good as the American four-wheeled wagons. The Japanese, however, had plenty of them and as a result were able to keep themselves well supplied.

The Russians used a two-wheel cart considerably larger than that of the Japanese, with flaring sides and ends. It was commodious and strong. The carts were drawn by shaggy Manchurian ponies of great strength and stamina. They moved faster than the Japanese horses that had to be led, and carried as much as 800 pounds over good roads and on short hauls, but a 500-pound load was normal. The carts were extremely serviceable, strong, light, and well constructed.

The British had an immense number of pack mules, small, active, vicious little beasts. They were led in tandem, three in one team, the halter chains of the two rear ones running into a ring in the side of

Supply and Transport on the March

the saddle of the preceding one. The coolie in charge of the three led the lead mule; he also took care of all three animals. The pack saddles were of iron or steel, very strong, light, and neat, with breast and breech strap. They had carved lugs or hooks on each side on which the load was hung. The parcels to be carried were lashed around with a close-twisted rope that was provided with small loops or ears, leather-covered to prevent chafing. To load the mule the cargo was simultaneously lifted to each side and the loops hung over the hooks. This was quick, but the load did not stay on if the mule trotted or acted up—as was frequently the case. In other words, the British lashed their loads to the saddle whereas the Americans lashed theirs to the mule. As the pack mules normally moved at the gait of the walking coolie, the system worked fairly well. The British also had a number of carts with wooden axles and solid wooden wheels. Many were abandoned along the line of march with broken axles and can only be regarded as a lumbering failure.

Later the British received a large number of carts from India. These were all steel with lattice bottoms and sides, patent hubs, wood felloes (rims) and spokes. They had a pole or shaft and were drawn by two pack mules, the pole being fitted with a swiveled crosspiece at its end. Each end of the crosspiece rested in the iron pack saddle, where it was engaged by a ring. The mule bridles were connected by a halter shank. The carts were well built and very strong and larger than the Russians', but the method of attaching the mules to the carts did not permit their full strength to be utilized. There was also considerable play to the saddle, causing sore backs on the animals even though the carts were lightly loaded. The British took excellent care of their animals; each was thoroughly groomed daily and blanketed at night. They were not only picketed with a heavy iron pin by the halter shank, but they had a heel loop or chain attached by a leather ring or collar, so that they were secured fore and aft. The English said it was impossible to picket them any other way because of their fighting propensities. They also said they could not drive them in the same manner as the American pack mules, although they admitted to not having tried it out.

The French, Italians, and Austrians had no transportation except what they picked up in China. The Germans were in practically the same situation, but they eventually received a large number of their military baggage wagons. These were narrow at the bottom and flared out widely at the sides. The axles were steel with a rectangular cross section and had no sand bars or false bolsters. The wheels were wood with patent hubs, and the spokes spaced very far apart, making a wheel too weak for a rough road. The absence of sand bars, together with the very narrow bottoms, concentrated the load on the center of the axles, causing many to buckle under the weight. This threw the wheels out of line and increased the drag on the team. Brake power was transmitted by a crank and rod fitted with a worm gear. The harness was made of leather, and breast straps were used instead of collars and hames. The man on the box drove only the wheel team. The lead team was controlled by a driver mounted on the near horse. This wagon did not compare with the American escort wagon. It was neither as strong nor as spacious and was badly shaped, and the system of driving required two teamsters instead of one.

All nations utilized native carts to supplement their transportation. These were of two kinds: the Peking carts used by the Chinese for passengers, and the huge, lumbering freight carts. The Peking cart consisted of a heavy pair of shafts mounted on an extremely heavy pair of wooden wheels with huge hubs, and a strong hardwood axle. Between the shafts was a light wooden platform; in some cases it was of woven rattan. It was surmounted by a latticework canopy covered with cloth and with a sunshade that extended over the cart mule. The vehicle was heavy, ungainly, and top-heavy. The freight cart was of the same general style except it had no top, but had a solid wood bottom, which made it heavier. In addition to the shaft animal there were three and sometimes four mules or ponies harnessed abreast with very long roped traces. These carts and animals carried enormous loads and were of great assistance to those troops whose own transportation facilities were limited. The province of Chihli was rich in ponies and mules that were ideal for pack mules because they were very short-coupled and had big barrels. Near Peking a large number of Bactarian (two-hump) camels were obtained. These ungainly creatures carried 500 pounds apiece and were the cheapest form of transportation in China. They ate all kinds of refuse forage that a mule would not touch and thrived on it. The saddle was simplicity itself, consisting of two narrow wooden bars running at right angles to the ribs. The cargo was merely tied together and hung on each side. One man cared for six animals. He led the first one by a long cord passed through the gristle of the nose; the other five were tied to their leaders in the same manner, with the cord being fastened to the saddle. The last camel carried a bell suspended from its neck, shaped like a section of stovepipe. As long as the bell sounded, the camel driver knew his string of animals was intact without looking around. The American troops used a number of these camels to haul coal. They had nasty tempers and were prone to kick

Supply and Transport on the March 137

and bite; many of them had to be muzzled. They were not satisfactory as saddle animals, having a motion similar to a Philippine coastal steamer in a typhoon.

All the foreign troops were very proud of their leather equipment. The British and Germans particularly kept theirs in beautiful condition. The Japanese marched with very little equipment, but they seemed to have everything they needed, and had no weight problem. The British troops were also lightly loaded; however, both the British and Japanese had a coolie for every fighting man, or about that proportion. The Russians carried very little—a rough blanket in a roll, the ends of which were tied together and stuck in their soup cans; a wooden water bottle and a canvas haversack completed their outfits. The French and Italians had heavy packs, and the Germans were very heavily loaded. They seemed to have a belt and pouch for everything from a pair of boots to a meerschaum pipe. It appeared that when they went into combat they would have to strip for action and run the risk of losing their packs, or else they would have to develop a strength and endurance that the other nations did not possess.

In the matter of dress, American soldiers were very sensibly clothed in comparison with the others, especially in the matter of foot and headgear. The Japanese limped in heavy, stiff brogans that they wore apparently for reasons of pride or "face," because they regularly marched barefoot or wore straw sandals in ease and comfort. Their summer uniform was of coarse white drill and so tight-fitting they looked ready to burst at every seam. Their winter uniforms were of coarse woolen cloth, varying in color and trimmings according to the organization. They were quite spectacular in their combinations. All the armies except the American reveled in color and gold lace in their winter uniforms, and although it was striking to the eye, their finery was also a nuisance because so much care and attention were required to keep it presentable. The American blue flannel shirts, however, received their share of admiration because of their quality.

Although the American troops were better fed, both in quantity and quality, better clothed, particularly for the winter, and had the best transportation, they did not measure up to the foreigners in military appearance. Our men were slouchy in dress and rambled about clothed, partially clothed, or dressed almost any old way their fancy dictated, and seemed to lack pride in their personal appearance. The foreigners thought this do-as-you-please manner was due to lack of discipline, whereas it was something of a national characteristic. And although it certainly existed in that era, the

Americans were always clean and their equipment was kept in good working order. The American fighting man could shoot better and take better care of himself than his more smartly dressed brothers-in-arms. Furthermore, he was animated by a spirit of humanity and regard for the rights of others that was in marked contrast to the actions of these same presumably better-disciplined European troops. He was also more self-sufficient.

The coolie camp followers accompanying the relief expedition were mostly with the British troops. Every two or three of the tall, turbaned British-Indian soldiers had a follower. Though the German, French, and English private had to take care of himself, the humblest of the black Mohammedans had at least half a servant to look after his belongings and carry them in a pack on his head. It was estimated that on the march there were 1,100 camp followers present with the British troops. They were also used to carry tents, camp equipment, stretchers, water, forage, fuel, and other supplies.

The Chinese did not volunteer for this service. A squad of soldiers would go anywhere to find them, round them up, and march them to camp. Most of them were desperately hungry. They were fed and put to work the next day. Being from the very poor class of Chinese, they appreciated having three meals a day. They were mostly naked above the waist; those who had shirts took them off to keep them clean and carried them in a roll under the end of a bamboo pole resting on the shoulder. A picturesque sight in one group that was marched in was a tall, dignified Chinese with an umbrella held high over his head during a heavy rain. He had no shirt and it was obvious that his straw sandals and tattered trousers had seen better days, but his dignity was intact. The coolies pressed into service with American troops were well treated and were paid twenty cents a day.

The Chinese coolies accepted their lot in a philosophical manner. They were taken involuntarily from their homes of a thousand years, desolated though they were, yet the coolies were quiet, calm, and serene, and on the whole did their work well.

And so the epic march began, with miles and miles of serving men, hundreds of them with big pigskins and leather bottles, accompanying the troops on their mission of mercy and duty.

Chapter X

The Relief of Peking and Paotingfu

Reconnaissance had shown that the Chinese occupied an intrenched position on both sides of the Pei Ho near Peitsang, where it was decided to assault and then push on to Yangtsun so as to secure the passage of the river at that important strategic point. It was generally agreed by the allies that the Japanese, English, and Americans were to operate along the right bank of the river, the other allies on the left bank.

Reports from Tientsin were that General Lung was at Yangtsun with about 10,000 men, while General Ma, the viceroy Yung Lee, and other officials of Tientsin were at Peitang with about the same number of troops. Russian and Japanese estimates of the strength of the enemy at Peitsang were 8,000 and 11,000 respectively. Both armies were said to be short of provisions and ammunition and greatly disheartened by their defeat. Information received from the General Staff at St. Petersburg was to the effect that the greater part of the defeated troops of Generals Lung and Ma were at Yangtsun with some of General Nieh's division, which had been dispersed, but that on the road to Peking and in the capital there were about 50,000 trained Chinese troops and large numbers of Boxers whose force was by no means broken.

As a result of the commanders' decision to start for Peking on August 4, the planned buildup of forces related in a preceding chapter never materialized. On August 31, after ample time to obtain the correct statistics, Reuters' Agency gave the numbers of the allied forces engaged in the relief expedition as follows:

Japanese: 6,600 infantry, 220 cavalry, 450 engineers, 53 guns.
Russian: 3,300 infantry, 180 cavalry, 22 guns.
British: 1,832 infantry, 400 cavalry, 13 guns.

American: 1,600 infantry, 75 cavalry, 150 marines, 6 guns.
French: 400 marines, 18 guns.
Total: 15,607 men, 112 guns.

The absence of Germans, Austrians, and Italians was explained by a telegram from Tientsin received in Berlin on August 11 that stated: "After the fight at Peitsang, the Germans, Austrians, and Italians returned to Tientsin, probably having no transportation for their supplies," and a telegram from General Frey, dated Tientsin, August 9, received at Paris, saying:

"Upon my return to Tientsin I offered the Germans, the Austrians, and the Italians, who are not at present represented in the column, to facilitate the dispatch of a detachment to cooperate, if necessary, in the capture in Peking. They accepted with gratitude, and the French forces, which had been left at Tientsin, are now making forced marches with them to join the column."

The number of guns with the expedition as tabulated above was in excess of the 70 agreed upon by the commander at the August 3 conference. The greater portion of the increase was due to the number taken by the Japanese. The British military attaché reported that they had 3 field batteries of 6 guns and 6 batteries of mountain guns, for a total of 54 guns. The French artillery was reported to have 2 mountain batteries firing melinite, and the Russians, 2 field batteries of 6 guns each.

The troops of each nation were under the control of their own commanders, who gave the necessary orders for carrying out the general plans and movements agreed to.

The American contingent, commanded by General Chaffee, was composed of the Ninth and Fourteenth Infantry regiments and Captain Reilly's Light Battery F, Fifth Artillery, totaling about 2,000 men. The Sixth Cavalry was left behind as a guard and was awaiting the arrival of its horses. The British forces, commanded by General Gaselee, consisting of 4 companies of the Royal Welsh Fusiliers, the First Bengal Lancers, First Sikhs, 250 men of the Twenty-fourth Punjab Infantry, and 400 men of the Seventh Bengal Infantry, the Twelfth Field Battery (6 guns), the Hong Kong Asiatic Artillery (2 naval 12-pounders and 4 Maxims), and the naval brigade (4 guns), about 400 strong (125 seamen and 278 marines).

The Japanese division was commanded by General Yamaguchi. General Fukishima was the chief of staff. The Russians, commanded by Lieutenant General Linievitch, had 2 regiments of infantry, nor-

The Relief of Peking and Paotingfu 141

mally of 2,000 men each but now under strength; 2 field batteries, and some Cossacks. The French, under General H. Frey, had about 400 men of the marine infantry from Cochin China, and 2 batteries of mountain guns.

The expedition got underway on the afternoon of August 4 when the Americans and British moved from camps and bivouacked at Hsiku; the Japanese followed and took a position in advance a little before midnight. The Russians and French were on the left side of the river and the Japanese were on the right side.

The general plan previously decided upon was followed. The Chinese position comprised a line of intrenchments running generally northeast and southwest, on both sides of the railroad. Their right rested on an embankment running westerly from Hsiku, and the left—nearly 5 miles away—at a camp near a railroad bridge beyond which the country had been flooded. The center had been greatly strengthened by a series of well-concealed rifle pits and trenches. From the river to their extreme right, where they had positioned a battery on the embankment, a single line of intrenchments

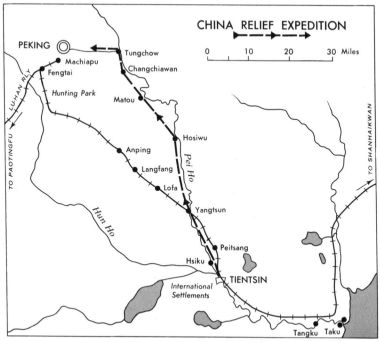

13. Route of the China Relief Expedition.

crossed the plain. On the other side of the river their position was strengthened by a canal running along its entire length.

The plans of the allies contemplated the turning of both flanks of the enemy's position. On the right bank the attack was to be made by the Japanese, supported by the Americans and British. Before daylight the whole force on the right bank moved forward to the west under cover of the embankment. About 3 A.M. the Japanese captured the battery on the embankment by a swift assault under brisk rifle fire, then drove in the enemy's right flank for some distance along their intrenchments. At daylight the artillery opened fire on the Chinese from behind the embankment. The artillery duel lasted about half an hour, when the Chinese fire slowed down and soon ceased entirely.

While it was in progress, the Japanese infantry, supported by a mountain battery on their right rear, had worked up close to the enemy's position on the river bank under cover of the high millet. A little after 5 A.M. they charged the enemy position in the face of severe fire from their front and heavy cross fire from the opposite side of the river. The enemy was driven from one intrenchment after another. Soon the entire force on the right side advanced, all crossing the protecting embankment and moving across the plain in open formation to the attack, with the Japanese advancing along the river, the British next, and the Americans on the left. The enemy did not wait and made almost no further resistance except for some occasional firing at long range from villages along the river.

The example of the flight from the first intrenchments was contagious, and the Chinese army retreated across to the left bank of the river toward Yangtsun. By 9 A.M all firing had ceased and Peitsang was occupied by the allies, where they halted, the task for the day having been completed. The casualty figures showed that the Japanese did almost all the fighting, and the credit for the victory was freely and cheerfully accorded them by the British and the Americans. The Japanese losses in the action were 60 killed and 240 wounded; the British, 1 killed and 25 wounded; the Russians, 6 wounded, the others had no casualties.

On the other side the Russians and French, with whom the British naval brigade was cooperating, were unable to outflank the Chinese position owing to the flooded conditions of the country. But the rout of the enemy by the Japanese compelled them to abandon their intrenchments, and the Russians and French moved up and occupied rout of the enemy by the Japanese compelled them to abandon their guns by withdrawing them early in the fight, except for the battery on the embankment, which was captured by the Japanese. This in all likelihood predisposed the rest of their army to its prompt retreat. The enemy did not suffer heavy losses. In the intrenchments near the river, where the Japanese had their greatest number of casualties, only a few Chinese dead were found. This was true of most of their line except on the extreme right where about 50 Chinese dead were counted.

The allies pushed forward for a mile or two after the retreating Chinese until stopped by the inundations. The enemy had cut the river bank at several points to flood the countryside. The allies then returned to Peitsang and, joined by the Russians and the French, all bivouacked for the night. Strong outposts were established 2 and 3 miles in advance. The halt at Peitsang was utilized to bring up supplies and prepare for the forward movement. The Americans had brought their own mules, which they handled with a skill and competence that was greatly admired. Many of the Japanese pack horses were stallions and were a constant source of trouble. The French had only a few small Annamite ponies, and, as has been noted, the Germans, Austrians, and Italians had none. The roads were really gullies, which in a hard rain soon turned into rivers of mud, and the intense heat took a heavy toll of the animals as time went on.

The plans for the next day, August 6, called for an early start. The Japanese were to continue marching on the right bank, repairing the breaks as they went forward. The rest of the allies were to move on the main road on the left bank of the river, with the Americans leading the advance. They were followed by the Russians and French, who clung to the river road, and they in turn were followed by the British, who, by marching on more direct roads, were able to pass them in a few hours and overtake the Americans. About 7:30 A.M. the advance element, a small party of Cossacks, made contact with the enemy. They occupied a strong position about 3 miles away in a group of villages situated in the angle made by the railroad embankment and the river. The ruins of the Yangtsun station on the left bank marked the approximate center of the position, their right being close to the river ending at a village and their left extending beyond the railroad among other mud villages.

Generals Chaffee and Gaselee made prompt dispositions for attack with one Russian battalion on the left, the British in the center, and the Americans on the right. The Twelfth Field Battery (British), supporting the left of the British line, commenced to shell the village in front of the railroad station. During the artillery fire the infantry reached the positions assigned them and deployed for the advance. The Ninth Infantry moved forward on the extreme right beyond the railroad embankment, supported by Reilly's battery, and was followed on their right rear by the First Bengal Lancers, assigned to operate on that flank. On the left embankment were the Fourteenth Infantry, then the British, the First Sikhs being on the front line supported by the Royal Welsh Fusiliers and the Twenty-fourth Punjab Infantry.

About the time that the dispositions were completed, General Linievitch arrived and stated that his troops were advancing on the left along the river embankment. The entire line now moved forward in regular order across the 5,000 yards of level plain, covered by the high millet that separated it from the enemy. They had covered nearly half the distance before encountering severe shell and rifle fire, from which the Fourteenth Infantry (U.S.) suffered the heaviest losses. The latter part of the advance was more rapid and irregular, and, when nearing the enemy, Colonel A. S. Daggett led his regiment in a charge across the remaining distance. The enemy broke and ran before the embankment was reached. The fight was won on that flank, and the position was occupied.

On the left the Russians had been fighting for two or three hours and, when the enemy retreated, they moved up a battery in rear of the captured village and shelled parties of Chinese who were retreating in all directions.

All the American forces were engaged in this assault, and it was to their excellent fighting qualities and drive that the allied success was primarily due. Their casualties show that the hardest of the fighting fell to their share. American losses in the Fourteenth Infantry were 10 killed and 55 wounded, with 9 wounded in the Ninth Infantry. The British commander officially acknowledged the valuable assistance rendered to his troops by Major Quinton and Captain Taylor of the Fourteenth. The British had 6 killed, 38 wounded, and one fatal case of sunstroke. Immediately after the fight the Russian commander reported that 2 of his men were killed and 116 wounded, but a later report listed 7 killed and 20 wounded.

The two-day march and fighting had been most fatiguing with its terrific heat and clouds of heavy dust on the treeless roads. The millet was tall enough but too thin to shut off the direct rays of the sun, and it extended for miles in all directions effectively cutting off any breeze, leaving the air still and loaded with dust particles raised by the moving troops and animals. All were so exhausted that it was decided to halt one day at Yangtsun to rest and bring up the supply trains.

When the expedition started from Tientsin, Yangtsun had been the immediate objective. Its position at the crossing of the river by the railroad made it a point of strategic importance in a march on the capital. The allied commanders held another conference there and agreed upon a definite order of march. All were to proceed on the right bank of the river, the Japanese leading, followed by the Russian, American, and British contingents in that order. The French remained in Yangtsun because of transportation problems.

On August 8 the relief expedition took to the road again. The fatigue and hardships of the march from Tientsin were many—heat and dust, scarcity of good water, inadequate supplies due to lack of transport—and unavoidable because of the necessity for haste. All the troops suffered the privations with patience and fortitude, if not with cheerfulness. The day's march brought the main body to Nantsaitsan, where it bivouacked for the night. Early the next morning the expedition renewed its march. The Japanese, who were still in advance, made contact with the enemy at Hosiwu and shelled that Chinese position. The Chinese were driven out, and the town occupied, before the main body of the allies arrived. The following day the troops reached Matow. It was not a great distance, about 12 miles, but conditions made it a most trying one. All the troops suffered, and there were numerous stragglers of every nationality along the line of march.

August 11 was somewhat cooler and a light rain shower brought welcome relief. The Japanese reached Changchiawan in the morning and, after making a strong reconnaissance, discovered the Chinese in a position about 3 miles south of Tungchow. They were driven out by artillery fire and retreated into the city.

Tungchow was now the only major obstacle between the relief expedition and Peking. It was a large depot for all kinds of supplies for Peking and, being a walled city, might have proved a formidable barrier to allied progress had it been properly defended. But early on the morning of the 12th, as the Japanese were preparing to attack, they found that it had been evacuated during the night and they were able to occupy the city without opposition. The French entered immediately after the Japanese. Being few in number and less burdened with impedimenta, they had been able to push on from Yangtsun and pass the rest of the allies.

The expedition was now within 12 miles of Peking, and plans and preparations were made for the attack. A conference was held on the 12th at which an advance in four columns was agreed on for the 13th. Each contingent was to concentrate about 5 miles from the walls of Peking, where another meeting of the commanders would be held to arrange the details for the attack to be made on the 15th. The American column was to advance on a line south of the canal running from Tungchow to the north gate (Tung Pien Men) of the city; the Russians were to pursue a parallel course on the north side of the canal; the British were to march to the south of the Americans; and the Japanese were to move parallel to the north of the Russians over the ancient stone causeway that ran to the eastern gate (Tsi Kwa Men).

The attack was precipitated on the 14th, however, when the Russians, instead of halting as agreed upon, continued their advance of the day before toward the walls. During the night they attempted to force the Tung Pien Men, which was to have been the American objective for the 15th. They were met by heavy fire and, becoming involved, had to continue to fight. When the other allies heard all the rifle firing, they realized the Russians had disregarded the agreement and had begun the assault single-handed, 24 hours earlier than the agreed time, and against the wrong objectives. Their conduct on the battlefield was severely criticized for these two breaks of compact. It was surmised by the other commanders that the Russians made the assault against the Tung Pien gate because it was the closest gate to the legations, and that General Linievitch hoped, by being the first to enter Peking, to reap the greatest honors. English and Japanese newspapers alleged that the time agreed upon by the allies for the attack had been anticipated by the Russians, who expected to enter the city with little if any fighting and thereby gain the prestige and any other advantages that would result from prior occupation of the city by their troops.

Nevertheless, all the other allies now joined in the attack, each advancing as rapidly as possible on the particular gate that lay in their line of march. The Americans' advance brought them to the Tung Pien, where the Russians were already engaged. They had advanced along the left of the canal under good cover. Captain Reilly's guns were shelling the Tsi Kwa gate from a hill affording a favorable position for this purpose and were assisting the Japanese in their attack on this gate. In the face of the fire of Chinese sharpshooters an American company scaled a corner of the wall by the Tung Pien gate about 11 A.M., then the Americans and Russians crowded through the gate into Peking, the former fighting their way westward, parallel with the wall from which the enemy had to be driven step by step.

The attacks by the Japanese, Russians, and Americans had the effect of concentrating the forces of the enemy to defend the threatened points. This left the east gate (Sha Wo Men) of the Chinese City free to be entered by the British, who had marched on the left of the allied columns. With the Americans fighting the Chinese on the wall, the British were able to move ahead without opposition and make their way through the water-gate under the wall to become the first to reach the legations. The Americans entered through the same passage an hour or so later, somewhat disappointed not to be the first group in, but rejoicing in the successful accomplishment of the objective of the expedition—the rescue of the legations.

The resistance at Tsi Kwa Men and Tung Chih Men to the Japanese attack was most obstinate, but was finally overcome at the Tsi Kwa gate some hours after dark at a cost of many casualties among the attacking force. The Japanese finally succeeded in blowing up the gate and setting the watch tower on fire. They rushed in with great enthusiasm in spite of heavy fire from the Chinese on the wall. Gaining the top, the Japanese infantry drove the enemy along the wall in the moonlight and fully avenged their own losses at the gate. The Russians likewise had a hard fight lasting fourteen hours at the Tung Pien gate and suffered heavy losses with 1 officer, Colonel Antinkoff, and 20 men killed, and 5 officers and 120 men wounded. American casualties were light; 8 were wounded in the Fourteenth Infantry, 1 in Battery F, and 1 officer and 2 men of the marines.

Many Chinese were still in the Imperial City, and the next day General Chaffee's command attacked and captured in succession the various gates, including the one giving access to the Forbidden City. It was entered at 3:30 P.M. by a company of marines, who hoisted their flag over one of the buildings. They remained there until 5:30 P.M., when they were ordered to withdraw, leaving a guard at the gate. This was the first and only occupation of the Forbidden City by the allied forces.

From the wall at the Chien Men, which had been held by the Americans overnight, Captain Reilly's battery shelled each of the great gateways. It was while directing these operations that he was killed. (See Chapter XI.) The withdrawal by General Chaffee from the Forbidden City was in deference to the sentiment that being the final evidence of victory, the occupation should be shared by all the allies. It may be questioned whether any of the other allied commanders would have shown the same self-restraint under the same circumstances. In other parts of the city the work of clearing out the enemy was going on, the Japanese and Russians operating on the east and to the north, and the British in the Chinese City to the south. The casualties of the Americans during the operations of the 15th were 7 killed and 19 wounded.

The most important task remaining to be accomplished, was the rescue of the Catholic missionaries and Chinese converts at the famous Peitang cathedral and mission, which was situated in the Imperial City near the west wall. On August 16 a combined Russian, French, and English force was organized to raise the siege of the Peitang. It moved out, encountered some resistance, and suffered some casualties in its progress. Before their arrival, however, the operations of the Japanese in the northwest portion of the city had practically ended the siege, but the French had the gratification of being actually the first to enter the defended enclosure where they received a heart-warming welcome from their fellow countrymen.

The question of the occupation of the Forbidden City was the subject of considerable deliberation by the allies, and it was discussed at several conferences of the commanders. On the one hand it was argued that if it were occupied, it would be such a desecration of the most sacred places of China that it could never be reoccupied by the Imperial court; whereas if it were not done, the whole lesson of the campaign would be lost on the Chinese, who would be led to believe that it was protected by their gods, and that the hated foreigners had really been, as usual, beaten by the invincible Chinese army.

In the vote that was taken on the question, Japan and the United States were opposed to the entry, but all the others approved it. It was agreed to make the formal entry at 8 A.M. on Tuesday, August 28. No cavalry or artillery were to take part mounted. Generals and their staffs were to ride horses, but no others. Troops would enter at the south gate, march through the north gate, and be dismissed. The question of the order of the march gave rise to a long discussion, the Japanese and Russian generals both claiming first place. General Linievitch proposed that the Japanese and Russians go in at the head side by side. General Fukishima said he would leave the matter to the final decision of General Yamaguchi. The latter eventually sent word that the Russians could go first. As in all probability there would be few if any spectators, there was little reason for insisting on the honors. The order of entry and the number of soldiers corresponding to each nation in the procession were then fixed as follows:

1. Russians   800
2. Japanese   800
3. English   400
4. American   400
5. French   400
6. German   250
7. Austrians   60
8. Italians   60

The Relief of Peking and Paotingfu   149

The French and German contingents were entirely out of proportion to the degree of their participation in the campaign. The French were very feebly represented in the attack on Peking, and the Germans were not there at all.

The Russians took entire charge of the ceremony of formal entry into the Forbidden City. It took place as planned except that the Austrians came last. The Russians had two bands, and the conduct, appearance, and marching of their men were good. The Japanese moved off promptly in their turn. They presented a uniform, neat, compact appearance. They marched with precision, using a sort of subdued goose step similar to the German step, with a full arm swing. The British troops, preceded by bagpipes and drums, were a composite body, all branches being represented. The marching of the American troops was reported to be as smart as any in the ceremony. The men seemed to be taller and slighter of frame than the European troops, but it should be remembered that the American wore better-fitting clothing and that their weight probably averaged 10 pounds below normal since they had just come up from a long period of service in the tropics. The American uniforms were the only ones bare of decorations. The absence of an American band was noticed, especially since the other bands were not provided with any of our national airs to play as the Americans marched. The Russian troops were drawn up in one of the interior courts and cheered the troops of the other nations as they passed by.

After the troops had been dismissed, the officers dismounted and inspected a number of buildings in a body. They were nearly all very dirty and dilapidated, both inside and out. No Chinese were found inside the palace except several hundred servants, eunuchs, etc. Though reluctant about opening the temples to foreigners, they were respectful, and no shots were fired. The whole ceremony was over in an hour.

Outside the palace there were some massive bronze dogs, 8 feet high, and some dragons, birds, and turtles also in bronze. The carvings on the marble steps were extremely fine. There were also many excellent old cloisonné objects in the temples and huge bronze vases outside. As a whole, however, the exhibition was exceedingly disappointing. The glories of the past had long ago departed, and the Chinese of the day were not even keeping clean the massive works of art left by their ancestors. The filth and decay prevalent in the heart of the Sacred Palace was regarded as a fair index of the condition of the Celestial Empire.

Paotingfu

Following the relief of Peking, the commanders of the international forces turned their attention to the organization of an expedition of English, French, German, and Italian troops to proceed from Peking to Paotingfu. No American troops were included in the expedition, but Captain Grote Hutcheson, Sixth U.S. Cavalry, was ordered to accompany the relief force in the capacity of an attaché or aide-de-camp on the staff of the commanding general, Sir Alfred Gaselee.

Captain Hutcheson's party consisted of 1 other officer, First Lieutenant G. Soulard Turner, Tenth U.S. Infantry, 2 mounted orderlies, 1 cook, and 1 civilian teamster. The party was furnished a good, serviceable, standard-pattern army wagon, a team of 4 mules, tentage, and other camp equipment, and carried supplies for 25 days. These arrangements enabled the party to be independent and able to care for itself, and it also relieved those with whom they were associated of all care for their welfare.

On October 12, 1900, the party proceeded from camp in the Temple of Agriculture in Peking to Changyantsuan, a small village some 4 miles south of Lukochow, where the forces were either in camp or billeted in the village. The expedition moved out the next morning and arrived at Paotingfu on October 19, after having remained in camp 11 miles away from its destination to rest for a day. The 92-mile distance was completed at an average of about 13 miles for each marching day.

The road was an ordinary dirt road that had been used for many years; it was, however, the main highway from Peking to southwestern China. The streams were generally spanned with heavy stone bridges, some perhaps a thousand years old, and one, known as Marco Polo's Bridge, at Lukochow was said to have been crossed by that celebrated traveler. They were all built alike, and, while many needed repairs, they were solid and enduring. There was a modern railroad bridge across the Pei Ho but no wagon bridges, so it was necessary to ford the river—which was practicable except immediately after heavy rains. In some places the road was paved with blocks of granite, but, like the bridges, it had not been kept in repair and many of the blocks were out of place and greatly worn, with deep ruts between blocks. These bad spots made travel difficult on the road but it was passable for the wagons and the artillery.

The countryside through which the expedition marched was flat and, except for a few groves here and there, almost treeless. The soil was generally sandy and highly cultivated. Since the harvest was almost completed, large quantities of forage were easily secured along the route of march, but the fields looked barren, almost with-

The Relief of Peking and Paotingfu 151

out any sign of vegetable life. The area was thickly populated, with villages about every mile.

During the march to Paotingfu the presence of the French flag was noticeable everywhere. Each village that was entered fairly blazed with them. Various explanations were offered for this display, but probably the real reason was a desire on the part of the French to establish prior occupancy in case of future diplomatic differences. Similarly the gates of the city were taken over by French troops before the arrival of the combined forces.

The military force marching from Peking, called Column B, was made up as follows:

> *Lieutenant General Sir Alfred Gaselee,* British Army (Indian contingent), commanding the expedition.
> *British force,* under Major General Richardson, included 4 squadrons of cavalry, 6 companies of infantry, ½ company of sappers and miners, and a battery of artillery, for a total complement of 1,215.
> *German force,* under Colonel von Normann, included 1 cavalry detachment, 2 battalions of infantry, and 2 batteries of artillery, for a total complement of 1,013.
> *French force,* under Colonel Lalubin, included 2 battalions of infantry and 1 battery of artillery, for a total of 950 men.

Thus the total effective force of Column B was 3,600 men.

The Tientsin column, Column A, was composed of the following troops:

> *General Bailloud* (French), commanding the entire column and the French troops.
> *French force,* consisted of 1 squadron of cavalry, 1 battery of artillery, between 2 and 3 battalions of infantry, and 1 pioneer section.
> *German-Italian* contingent, under General von Kettler, included: German force, 1 troop of cavalry, 1 battery of artillery, 2 battalions of infantry, and 1 field hospital.
> Italian force, 1 battery of artillery, 2 companies of infantry, 1 detachment of engineers, and 1 baggage detachment.
> *British force,* General Lorne--Campbell commanding, (General Pipon commanding the artillery): 1 troop of cavalry, 1 battery and 2 detachments of artillery, 1 battalion and 11 companies of infantry, and sappers and miners.

The actual strength of all units in the Tientsin column is not known, but it was estimated at about 3,600 effective men.

A small part of the relief expedition, French troops claiming to be a reconnaissance party, had proceeded to Paotingfu considerably in advance of the main column, arriving there as early as October 12. Later, about October 15, this detachment was reinforced by other French troops until the total strength was about 400 men. They did not enter the city, but took possession of the four gates.

The Tientsin force marched in 3 columns on parallel roads, the troops of each nation making up a separate force except for the Italians who marched with the Germans. On October 18 the commanding general of the Tientsin column (General Bailloud) reported to General Gaselee at Anshu, where arrangements for proceeding to Paotingfu were completed. The following day the entire expedition moved toward its objective.

Just before the column reached Paotingfu, General Gaselee was met by a large delegation of Chinese officials from the city, led by Ting Yung, the fantai, or provincial treasurer. The delegation had proceeded several miles from the wall on the north road for the purpose of showing the readiness of the officials to turn the city over to the combined foreign military forces without opposition and to extend a welcome to all soldiers and an invitation to consider themselves guests of the city. They offered certain gifts, which were declined, and stated that certain general arrangements had been made to provide some of the troops with food and shelter. They also expressed the hope that the troops might be kept out of the city because they were fearful that it would be sacked and burned.

Little was replied to the delegation. General Gaselee stated that the expedition's actions would depend upon circumstances and that he would deal only with the highest official.

Upon arrival at the city it was observed that the gates were held by French troops under the command of Colonel Droude. They had arrived there seven days earlier and taken possession of the gates. General Gaselee rode to the north gate but did not enter. Inside were some Chinese soldiers, but they had no arms. Immediately thereafter a conference of the allied military commanders was held, and it was decided not to enter the city that afternoon. The English and French agreed, but the Germans protested the decision. Nevertheless, all troops made camps outside the walls. At a second military commanders' conference that day it was decided to enter the city formally at 10 A.M. the following day, October 20, and that the procession was to be made up of the various commanding officers with small staffs and escorts.

The Relief of Peking and Paotingfu   153

Accordingly, the entry was made the next morning, and the four flags of the nations represented by a military force (English, French, German, and Italian) were placed side by side over the four gates. The city was divided into four quarters, and one gate was given to each nation to guard—north to the English, south to the Italians, east to the Germans, and west to the French. It was also decided to move general headquarters into the city. The next day, October 21, General Gaselee, with his staff, occupied the Liang-Chiang-Hui-Kwan, or the Guild of the Provinces of Chiangsu and Chiangsi, one of the most important places in the city, where he remained during his stay at Paotingfu.

It was further decided to take formal military possession of the city. A military chief of police was appointed, and the city was divided into four military districts, one of which was assigned to each nation for guard, protection, policing, and the quartering of troops if desired. The Germans, French, and Italians, in whole or in part, quartered their men in their respective districts, but the English troops remained in camp outside the walls, merely detailing in the city enough men to maintain the necessary guards. By the evening of October 22 all these changes were in effect.

About this time it was reported that the French and Germans intended to occupy the city with a considerable force during the winter, and that the French were anxious to preserve the city from pillage and destruction. They had already taken charge of the railroad and were pushing repairs. The buildings, shops, and tracks at Paotingfu had suffered but little damage during the summer, and the road south to Tingchow, about 40 miles, was and had been in continuous operation. Little work remained to be done to make the line serviceable to the terminus at Chengtingfu—only laying the ties and the rails. The railroad was being repaired by railroad company employees under the protection of French troops. It was expected that service would be established between Paotingfu and Peking within four to six weeks.

An inquiry into the harsh, cruel, and inhuman treatment of foreigners during the past summer was begun as soon as the expedition reached Paotingfu on October 18, and all manner of stories were repeated by various Chinese witnesses. The actions of the Chinese, both officials and inhabitants, seemed generally so shameful that it appeared additional punishment should be meted out. On October 20 General Gaselee spoke to Captain Hutcheson about the matter and asked his opinion as to the punishment of the guilty. He also inquired about what General Chaffee's action might be under the circumstances, and how the United States might view his procedure or that of the combined military commanders. He specifically wished to know their attitude, since more Americans had suffered and been murdered in Paotingfu than any other nationality.

Captain Hutcheson replied that "no special power had been delegated" to him and that he could scarcely presume to speak for his commander, but that:

(1) In his opinion "the United States would uphold the prompt punishment of any officials whose guilty connivance was clear and plain, provided such punishment was meted out for the purpose of example and not to satisfy any petty feeling of revenge or retribution."

(2) That any steps General Gaselee thought necessary and proper under the circumstances would in his opinion meet the approval of and be endorsed by General Chaffee; and

(3) That in view of the tense feeling because of the stories of atrocious treatment and brutal murder of missionaries that had come to light, he suggested that a commission or board of inquiry should be instituted to make an impartial examination into the conduct of the officials and any other accused persons, and whose report and recommendation might serve as a basis for action.

General Gaselee had already thought of this last procedure, and on October 21 an international commission was created to inquire into the treatment of the foreigners of various nations at Paotingfu. It was composed of:

> General Bailloud, French Army, President
> Colonel Ramsey, British (Indian) Army
> Lieutenant Colonel Salsa, Italian Army
> Major von Brixen, German Army
> Mr. J.W. Jamison, civilian, British consul at Shanghai

Mr. Jamison, who was with the expedition, had an intimate knowledge of the Chinese language and of the customs and character of the Chinese people.

The international commission held daily sessions until October 27, when it ended its principal investigations. The following recommendations were formally endorsed by General Gaselee and sent to Field Marshal Count von Waldersee for final action:

The following Chinese officials were recommended to be put to death by the Chinese method used for criminals—beheading: Ting Yung, formerly the provincial treasurer and at the time of the murders of the missionaries the provincial judge; Quei Heng, the chief Tartar official of the city and one of the most prominent men to offer moral, financial, and official aid to the Boxer movement; and Wang

Chan Kuei, a lieutenant colonel in the Chinese army and the military commander of the cavalry camp opposite the east gate of the city where the Bagnell family went and were refused refuge, and by whom their silver and other valuables were stolen.

Shen Chia Pen, the provincial judge who was prefect of the city at the time of the murders, was recommended to be degraded, removed from office, and held at Paotingfu under military restraint until his replacement arrived.

T'an Wen Huan, then taotai, who was alleged to have sent money and arms from Tientsin for Boxers at Paotingfu, was recommended to be sent to Tientsin for trial.

The board further recommended that the gates of the city be destroyed, that all pagodas and other buildings on the walls be burned, and that the southeast corner of the city wall be demolished. On October 27, in accordance with General Gaselee's orders, certain public places were blown up and destroyed:

Cheng-Huang-Miao Temple. This was the temple of the tutelary divinity of the city and was considered especially precious. Its destruction was a blow to the pride of the people and its loss was viewed as a disaster and a punishment to the entire city.

Chi-Sheng-An Temple. This temple, one of the Boxer headquarters, was in the southeast part of the city and the place where Miss Morell, Miss Gould, and the Bagnell family were interrogated and held by the Boxers for some hours prior to their murder.

A list of 12 or 15 temples was submitted by the English with the request that they be destroyed during the winter by troops occupying Paotingfu. Approximately 2,000 Germans and 1,200 French were left when General Gaselee's international force started back to Peking on October 29. Whether all these other temples actually were destroyed during the winter was not made a matter of record.

Chapter XI

Reilly's Battery in China

On July 9, 1900, Captain Reilly received General Orders No. 49 from Headquarters, Division of the Philippines, Manila, to prepare Battery F for movement to China. Immediately there was a beehive of activity, with some government property to be turned in and other property, supplies, and equipment drawn preparatory to the voyage and for service in China. The battery, 5 officers, 146 enlisted men, 96 horses, 8 mules, 6 guns, 9 caissons, 1 battery wagon, and 2 escort wagons, and part of the Fourteenth Infantry were loaded on the transport *Flintshire*. The vessel had been designed to carry freight and animals, consequently the accommodations for officers and men left much to be desired. At 9:15 A.M. on Sunday, July 15, the ship weighed anchor and steamed away from Manila.

By Tuesday morning the transport was just a trifle north of the northern point of Luzon, heading a little east of north so as to pass east of the island of Formosa. At twilight the next night the ship passed a great rock called Ralaigh, standing alone in the vast ocean. Twilight was noticeable because in Manila there was little dusk and the darkness came on suddenly. On Saturday the 21st the transport arrived at Nagasaki, Japan. While there the battery surgeon, Dr. Greenleaf, son of the Surgeon-General, Lieutenant McCloskey, and a few officers of the Fourteenth Infantry went ashore, "got into those funny jin-rick-shaws and saw a Geisha dance, drank tea and came back on board on a little sampan. The dance was by little girls, twelve or thirteen, dressed very fancifully but I (Lieutenant McCloskey) was not much impressed." The quotes in this chapter are taken from Lieutenant McCloskey's letters home. Apparently, no matter how weary at the end of a long day, the young Lieutenant managed to write frequently to his financée and family, who carefully preserved them.

At 9:30 A.M. on Tuesday, July 24, the vessel weighed anchor and steamed out of Nagasaki. The weather was fresher and cooler and the salt air invigorating, but the poor horses were tired and worn out and obviously anxious to plant their feet on solid ground. During the stay in Nagasaki the ship was refueled by low-caste coal heavers. "Men, women, boys, and girls, some very old, some but infants, helped in the coal heaving. They began at seven and worked till six with only a few short rests—it was wonderful to see them, covered with dust so that you could not distinguish their features, working so happily. All about Nagasaki the women work just as men. When they worked on the vessel at night, the women wore only that head cloth to protect their hair and a short skirt without any waist—they were not pretty—the men wore a shirt and a breech cloth in the day but doffed the shirt at night. Such dirty people I never saw before. Ladders were built from the coal boat to the upper deck and the coal is handed in little baskets from step to step."

On July 27, the *Flintshire* reached the harbor at Taku. "We came within sight of the great fleet anchored here about five o'clock yesterday afternoon. Of course we all crowded to the rail and scanned the view with our glasses. Such a sight I had never seen—such a vast fleet of vessels. They were of every nation and of every description. There were great massive battle-ships, cruisers, armored and unarmored, torpedo boats, transports for men, transports for horses, hospital ships, merchant-men—the number was over fifty and in addition there were launches, tenders, junks and lighters without number. It was a grand sight. The flags of Japan, Russia, England, Germany, France and our own were most conspicuous.... It is nine o'clock now and the harbor is aglow with the lighted vessels. The harbor is only a part of this Gulf of Pechili and is no harbor as you understand the word. We are all from eight to ten miles from the shore, Taku, and cannot get closer without grounding. Our landing place is fourteen miles from this ship."

The following day the baggage and supplies were brought up from the hold to the vessel's upper deck before off-loading onto river boats, barges, and lighters. Lieutenant Summerall was put in charge of transferring the ammunition from the ship to the lighter *Pechili*, while Lieutenant McCloskey had charge of removing the guns, tents, and harness from the hold and loading them onto a sort of barge. Work began at 8 when the *Pechili* and the barge came alongside. It was raining and a cold wind was blowing. By 10 o'clock all the personnel were cold and drenched to the skin. "The sea blew up very rough and the men working in the little lighter alongside, packing the guns, got seasick from the pitching and tossing of the little craft. The rain just poured down."

Extracts from official messages indicate that the off-loading of the entire battery to the river craft and then to shore was an arduous and time-consuming task:

Chefoo, China (Received July 30, 1900, 11:30 P.M.
Adjutant-General, Washington:
Have had interview with admiral. Go ashore this afternoon. Facilities for unloading not adequate; therefore discharging slowly. Informed Byron has ordered tug for towing two 70-ton lighters. If tug is obtained, discharging will improve. . . . Take two days to unload horses Reilly's battery. . . .

CHAFFEE

* * *

War Department, Washington August 2, 1900
To the Secretary of the Navy.
Sir: In view of the great difficulties of landing troops, animals, and munitions of war at Taku, I beg to suggest that you should send specific instructions to the admiral commanding the fleet at that point to render all assistance possible by the use of both men and material to expedite such landing, and also in transportation as far as practicable upon the River Peiho.

Very respectfully,
ELIHU ROOT
Secretary of War

* * *

Chefoo, China (Received August 3, 1900—2:15 P.M.)
Adjutant-General, Washington:
Tientsin, 31 July. Do not believe ministers can be relieved without overthrow of Chinese troops intrenched between here and Pekin. An aggressive step probable August 3. Objective, Yangtsun or crossing of railway to right bank river 25 miles from here. . . . Bay so rough yesterday and to-day little accomplished unloading. Battery and cavalry still on ship. Quartermaster stated everything working night and day. . . .

CHAFFEE

* * *

Navy Department,
Washington, August 3, 1900

The Secretary of War.
Sir: Replying to the letter of the War Department, dated August 2, requesting the assistance of Admiral Remey in landing troops at Taku, the Department informs you that it has this day cabled Rear-Admiral Remey in the following words:
"Render all assistance possible, with men, boats, and material to aid

landing of troops, animals, ammunition at Taku and transportation as far as practicable upon the Peiho."

I have the honor to be, sir, very respectfully,

F. W. HACKETT
Acting Secretary.

Before arriving in China, Lieutenant McCloskey had already demonstrated the qualities of leadership, imagination, and practical wisdom that had gained the respect and confidence of his superiors, his colleagues, and his men. He had that rare quality of greatness that is sensed but cannot be defined. It .consisted partly of humor, immense common sense, and the power to concentrate on one or two pertinent points. But there was something more than any separate quality—that indefinable something that one just feels about certain people the moment they enter a room. Lieutenant McCloskey was one of those people. In later years he was always a center of attraction wherever he went, and the stories that he loved most to narrate were about Reilly's Battery. Though half the charm was in his telling, here is the story compiled from his letters and diaries and the history handwritten by the anonymous battery historian.

The six guns of Reilly's Battery had been well secured on a 70-ton barge and were at last under way for Taku. Up ahead, practically invisible in the darkness and the stormy weather, the tug churned away. Suddenly there was a loud report as if one of the 3.2-inch guns had been fired. The long, heavy towline had parted, and the Navy tug vanished into the night. The barge, released from its tug, floundered helplessly in the churning waters of the Gulf of Pechili. The artillerymen traveling on the barge with the guns referred to their sister service in terms familiar only to artillerymen and mule skinners— they were anything but complimentary. For almost a month the soldiers had been living under miserable conditions, been seasick in the rough storms, fought a fire in a coal bunker near thousands of rounds of ammunition—and now this! The American Expeditionary Force of 1900 was about to lose its artillery to Davy Jones' locker.

Trying to use a rammer staff as an oar, a veteran sergeant regretted profanely that Captain Reilly was not with them. The Captain, who had seen service in 1861 on a Union gunboat on the Mississsippi, would know how to get them out of this predicament. Unfortunately Captain Reilly was not there; he had gone ashore with the horses. But among those on the barge was a tall, thin young stowaway who had been discovered aboard the transport. He was enlisted on the spot by Lieutenant Summerall, who had a hunch that he might prove useful. The artillery recruit hesitantly informed the irate sergeant, in tones of one confessing his sins of the past, that he had once been a sailor. "What are you waiting for," roared the sergeant. "Get to sailing!"

A search of the barge's various lockers revealed two sails; the mast was stepped and a rudder fabricated, and the craft came under control. The seaman-soldier sailed his barge in circles all during a cold, weary, sleepless night to remain in the same general area. At daybreak a small British customs boat came within hailing distance. Luckily it had a pilot on board to guide the barge across the dangerous bar of the Pei Ho, passing the battered forts of Taku within sniffing distance of the stench that reeked to high heaven arising from the decaying corpses of the Chinese killed during the bombardment by the foreign navies. At last a safe landing was made and the guns were run ashore. Another lap, close to being the last one, had been completed in the race to rescue the beseiged legations.

Captain Reilly was waiting impatiently at the war-torn town of Tangku. He worked off some of his impatience by grooming his own horse, as was his custom; some of it he took out on the drivers whose lead, swing, or wheel teams failed to have coats shining like satin. Aided by some 200 Chinese coolies, the guns, ammunition, supplies, wagons, and horses were loaded on the trains. The teams remained in harness so that the battery could be unloaded and go quickly into action if necessary. The trains looked like the Chinese equivalent of the French "40 hommes, 8 chevaux" of World War I.

Captain Reilly and Lieutenant McCloskey, with the cannoneers and guns, left Tangku on August 2 on the first train for Tientsin. Lieutenant Summerall, with the remainder of the battery and the horses, followed on a second train. Throughout the night the trains rattled along, making many stops on the precarious right of way, carrying to the combat area an organization that was destined to be outstanding in the annals of artillery history. The platoons, led by the young lieutenants and composed of veteran noncommissioned officers and soldiers hardened and experienced by the campaigns in the Philippines, commanded by one officer, the redoubtable Captain Reilly, achieved a reputation and tradition of success in combat in the Old Army that has seldom been equaled. Each gun of Reilly's battery was an infantry support weapon, and invariably the guns would be found with the leading troops of the advance parties in combat. Captain Reilly was one of the greatest artillerymen of the Old Army and he became famous for his philosophy, "Gentlemen, there must never be anything to explain in the battery."

At Tientsin the battery was swiftly unloaded. Horses and men alike had had enough of traveling through tumultuous seas and in jolting railroad cars. They were all happy to be mobile again under their own power. While the battery detrained and the animals were fed, watered, and groomed, Captain Reilly reported to General Chaffee. He returned shortly with his orders. General Chaffee had been holding up the China Relief Expedition until the arrival of the battery. Mounted and facing his men, Captain Reilly raised his extended arm from shoulder height to overhead—the signal for drivers and cannoneers to mount. Moving as one man, the drivers swung up into their saddles and the cannoneers onto their limber seats. At 2 P.M. on August 4 at Reilly's command, "Forward, Haooooo!" the battery moved out with the Captain at its head as always.

Lieutenants Summerall and McCloskey and First Sergeant Follinsby commanded the three platoons. Lieutenant Burgess rejoined the battery after the battle of Yangtsun on August 6 and resumed command of the right platoon, and Lieutenant McCloskey resumed command of the center platoon. In the meantime, Sergeant Follinsby also checked on the battery's recruits to make sure that they appreciated the honor of wearing the redleg uniform.

The battery marched past the battle-scarred walls of Tientsin. The Chinese portion of that city was completely wrecked. The houses were full of bullet holes, woodwork splintered by artillery, great holes in brickworks, and everything bore the marks of heavy infantry and artillery fire. Many houses were practically burned down, the roofs and walls caved in with everything inside entirely destroyed. The area was devoid of human life, but the decaying corpses of dead Boxers were everywhere in evidence.

Marching to take their position in General Chaffee's column, the battery rolled past the U.S. Marines under Major Waller. "The Marines had a warm feeling for the redlegs, cheering them as they moved ahead. Past Troop M of the Sixth Cavalry, the twelve companies of the Ninth Infantry and the eight companies of the Fourteenth Infantry, Captain Reilly led his battery. The cheers of the doughboys as the battery rolled ahead brought forth wide grins of appreciation and many a lump in the artillerymen's throats. No greater tribute could be paid to the battery than to hear the infantry shouting, 'Make way for the guns!'

"General Chaffee's American contingent of about 2,000 joined the 20,000 men of the International Relief Force Expedition. It was not exactly a formidable force and it was going into the dragon's den to fight not only the Boxers but also the armies of Imperial China. Admiral Seymour's Relief Expedition of June 1900 was almost crushed to death in the coils of the Chinese dragon." Rumors, true and false, circulated in the international force, and as time went on the reports were magnified: The legation defenders had been overcome and all was lost; the defenders were still holding out, but it was just a question of time until they would be overcome by the Chinese onslaught; there was no doubt but that the International Expedition would one day capture Peking, but would it be soon enough?

Frequently the drivers and cannoneers marched along the side of the road to make the going easier on the artillery teams. Suddenly they were at Peitsang, and the rifle firing of the Japanese advance guard was heard. The fighting had now become general, and judging by the number of casualties, it was heavy fighting. The assault on Peitsang was no pushover. Captain Reilly's men were eager to get their 3.2-inch guns in the fighting and they knew their Captain would see to it that they did. That night, August 4, they camped at Sin Ho, but at 4 A.M. the next day they went into action with the Ninth and Fourteenth Infantry and U.S. Marines who were supporting the assaulting Japanese and English forces up the Pei Ho.

Captain Reilly galloped from one spot to another seeking the most favorable location for his guns. Selecting his position, he gave his orders; the battery trotted smartly "front into line"; another order, and the battery executed the "action front maneuver" whereby the six guns and six caissons were unlimbered and prepared for action while the limbers were galloped a short distance in rear. Captain Reilly issued his firing instructions. The gunners carefully sighted on the parapets of a fort, behind which the Chinese with their banners, pikes, rifles, and guns fired at the Americans. At the Captain's command, "Commence firing," shell and shrapnel began to sweep the crests of the parapets, and above the din of conflict the artillerymen could hear the screams of pain and cries of surprise as those of the Boxers who could fled from the fort. The U.S. Infantry charged the enemy positions and the village was captured.

On the following day, the 6th, the battery marched to Yangtsun and from 11 A.M. to 2:30 P.M. was fighting the enemy. The day was a scorcher. Men's lips grew parched and their tongues so swollen they could scarcely speak. The local wells were reported to be poisoned and so were useless. The hot Chinese sun was far worse than anything the troops had had to put up with in the Philippines, and what little breeze might spring up was deflected by the tall millet through which the troops advanced. Spearheading the assault was the Fourteenth Infantry, with Reilly's guns in the advance party supporting the doughboys just as they had in the Philippine campaigns. There was a saying in the Fourteenth that no gun of Reilly's would ever be lost as long as there was a squad of the Fourteenth left, and that the Fourteenth would never go under as long as Reilly had a gun and a round of ammunition left.

Captain Reilly continued his characteristic practice of galloping the battery from position to position, shelling any concentration of enemy forces and any defensive position manned by the enemy that might hinder the advance of the infantry. The sweltering sun finally set, and the exhausted troops and animals came to a halt. Although the muddy water of the Pei Ho was foul with floating bodies, men and animals quenched their thirst in it. At dawn the column of the international force resumed their race against time to Peking. Captain Reilly's artillerymen, walking beside their teams and limbers, admired the advance party of colorful Bengal lancers as they rode forward through the millet fields; but their admiration turned to disgust as they watched the turbaned horsemen beat a hasty retreat to the main body at the first contact with scattered Chinese rifle fire.

As the days rolled by it was a steady diet of marching, fighting, marching, fighting for the battery. And the guns were always in close contact with the infantry. As in the Philippines, the guns were fired singly, in salvos, and in volleys.

At the Pei Ho crossing, the battery was forced to halt because a column of Russian infantry had started to march across the bridge. Riding ahead to the column's commanding officer, Captain Reilly courteously requested permission to pass through the Russian troops. The artillerymen, watching for the signal to move out, saw the Russian commander shake his head. An artillery section leader commented, "There must be loot in the next village!" A few more words were exchanged between the two commanders. The waiting artillery men saw Captain Reilly straighten in his saddle and take a hard look at the American infantry in action across the river. The next moment he wheeled his horse around to face the battery. He barked out a sharp command, and the Czar's foot troops scattered hastily as the artillery drove through the column. One of the drivers of a big wheel team shouted to the other drivers on his gun, "To hell with diplomacy" as his horse jolted a stubborn Russian soldier out of the way into the railing of the bridge. The battery was soon in position supporting the infantry.

General Chaffee's Relief Expedition had started out on August 4 and, if its luck held out, it might reach Peking by the 13th or 14th. Hopefully it would not be too late. Rumors circulated that there were thousands of troops in position to defend the next objective, the town of Yangtsun. Marching through millet fields and over narrow, crooked, winding roads, the international columns began to converge on the town. Skirmishers of the advance parties drew heavy Chinese fire as they made contact with the enemy. The assaulting forces were held back until the British and Japanese artillery were in position and returning the fire of the Boxers' guns. Even as Captain Reilly was leading his battery forward through the six-foot high millet, he was ordered to go into action against the guns of the Chinese.

The tall grain stalks concealed the movement of the battery as it maneuvered into position, but they also prevented the gunners from seeing the targets through the gun sights. That did not slow down the artillerymen. An observation ladder was unstrapped from a caisson, and mounting it step by step until he could see the targets, Lieutenant Summerall called out the firing data. His position, however, worked both ways, for every Chinese with a rifle in the immediate front drew a bead and fired at the foolish white foreign devil so clearly visible above the millet. Fortunately they were not good marksmen, and in a few moments the platoon's shell and shrapnel began bursting on top of them. Not far away, Lieutenant McCloskey stood on a caisson in his platoon. He knew he was similarly vulnerable to enemy rifle fire, but he called down the fire control data, directing his platoon's firing. Soon the Chinese guns ceased firing, and the American Fourteenth Infantry charged in with bayonets.

The fierce, scorching sun parched the men's lips and again created an agonizing thirst that was made worse by the sight of the wells they had to pass up because of the suspected poisoning. Finally, after much precious time was spent marching and fighting, the international force came within striking distance of Peking. As the Chinese retreated they left pikes sticking up along the sides of the roads, on top of which they placed the bloody heads of recently murdered Chinese Christians. It was at Tungchow on August 12, just 13 miles from Peking that at a conference of the four commanders, the details and arrangements for attacking Peking in four columns on August 15 were agreed upon.

But as the artillerymen tossed and turned in their pup tents on the night of the 13th, they were awakened by the sound of gunfire coming from the direction of Peking. Were the Boxers putting on a final drive to wipe out the legations? By the time Captain Reilly returned from General Chaffee's headquarters, where he learned that the Russians had jumped the gun on the allies and had moved on Peking during the night, the artillerymen had broken camp, taken care of the animals, and were standing by, ready to move. By daylight the battery was well down the Grand Canal Road, and the Great Wall of Peking was clearly visible.

"The sense of urgency, and the feeling that the battery was about to participate in an operation that would become renowned forever in history seemed to be shared by the horses and men alike. And Putnam, the near wheel horse of a gun section, made a little history himself that day. As his team turned out of the deep cut in the road, he threw himself into the draft with the other horses to pull the gun up a steep bank into position to fire. The drivers, leaning forward in their saddles, talked to their pairs, encouraging them to pull harder as they struggled up the bank. They were almost on top when the trace springs snapped under the tremendous strain, and of the six horses only Putnam was still hitched to the gun. The mighty wheel horse threw his shoulders against the collar and there on the steep grade, he, and he alone, held the limber and the attached gun from rolling backwards and dragging the other horses into a bloody, tangled heap at the bottom. For just a fraction of a second he braced himself, then with another herculean effort he lunged forward, pulling the limber and gun up onto the high ground. (Note: Seven years later when I was again stationed in the Philippines, I obtained Putnam's retirement from active battery service in memory of his heroic achievement, and the grand old horse spent his remaining years pensioned in a pasture.)"

The battery first went into action about 3,200 yards from the tower of the wall at the southeast corner of Tartar City. Lieutenant Burgess, grinning like a boy with a new toy, called out the firing data to the right platoon. It was not often that an artilleryman had a pagoda for a target. His absence from the battery on staff duty had not impaired his efficiency. His two guns fired twenty rounds into the pagoda, which burst into flames.

With the anger of men who had been tricked by the Russians, and with the abandon of soldiers who feared they might be too late, the American forces hurled themselves on Peking. An intrepid squad of the Fourteenth Infantry scaled the wall and planted the Stars and Stripes, the first foreign flag to wave over the wall. Lieutenant Summerall's platoon began firing on the enemy when it was just a mile from Peking. The remainder of the battery advanced along the road to the corner of the wall of the Chinese City and Tartar City. Under the heavy fire of Chinese riflemen, the Russian column, which had started out the night before, had been stopped. Unable to advance—or retreat—the Russians had unhitched their teams and left their guns effectively barring the entrance to the Tung Pien gate.

There was no conference between the commanders this time. The tough American cannoneers of Summerall's platoon shoved the Russian guns to one side, then pushed two unlimbered guns forward through the column of the Czar's infantry. A house that blocked their advance was torn down by the gun crews on Captain Reilly's

14. *A gun of Reilly's Battery in action in Peking.*

order and leveled close enough to the ground that the guns had a clear field of fire. The gunners sighted their targets and the platoon commenced firing. Their shells crashed into the pagoda, soon silencing the enemy fire. The U.S. Infantry and Reilly's battery charged ahead rapidly. "The Russians had jumped the gun but they hadn't won the race—and the rescue of the beseiged legations was so near —if it weren't too late."

Although the three platoons of the battery were separated to supone shot of 20 failing to enter a window. The interior of the tower was built of very old dry timbers, floors and uprights, and burned that day and the next, having been very probably ignited by the shell fire of the platoon. Gen. Chaffee personally gave the order to commence and to cease firing. The platoon then advanced with Gen. Chaffee & staff & the 9th Inf. to the Ha Ta Men. Here two shell were fired to break thro a portcullis and this failing, the gate was raised about 18 inches from the ground showing other gate beyond. Gen. Chaffee having moved on, the platoon followed along the south wall of the Tartar City, & halted while the Gen. entered the city thro the sluice gate with the British. Then the platoon joined the right platoon and camped for the night.

On the morning of Aug. 15th the center platoon was designated to fire from the top of the wall by the Chien men. The cannoneers prepared the long ramp leading up the wall which had not been used by vehicles for many years, ten horses were hitched to each piece, the cannoneers had hold of the wheels, and the pieces were soon on the top of the wall pointing westward to the Shun Chin gate, a mile distant, from which an annoying inf & arty fire was delivered in spells by the Chinese. This fire was silenced by the platoon, altho with some difficulty, because of the strong cover afforded the Chinese by the crennellations of the wall.

Then occurred the unutterably sad death of

15. A page from Lieutenant McCloskey's diary.

port the assaulting infantry companies to which each was assigned, Captain Reilly was in constant touch with them and controlled their operations. Lieutenant Summerall moved his platoon across the Tansang bridge into the Chinese City, where it went into position to shell the east and south walls of Tartar City. Lieutenant Burgess received heavy enemy fire from the south wall of Tartar City near the Ha Ta gate while moving through the Chinese City. He fired several shots into the wall and went up to and entered the Chien gate. From there he fired several rounds into the gate of the Imperial City. "After entering the Chinese City I advanced my platoon along the south wall of the Tartar City until within about 400 yards of the Ha Ta gate. About twenty shells were fired into the gate and the gate tower. The two guns were placed side by side in a narrow street and began to fire thorite and common shell into the three rows of windows in the stone tower surmounting the gate. The gunners' work was excellent, only one shot of 20 failed to enter a window. The interior of the tower was built of very old, dry timbers, floors and uprights, and burned that day and the next, having been very probably ignited by the shell fire of my platoon. General Chaffee, who was on the roof of a large building, was in communication with the beseiged legations. Gen. Chaffee personally gave the order to commence and to cease firing." The platoon then advanced with General Chaffee, his staff, and the Ninth Infantry to the Ha Ta gate. Here two well-aimed shells blew up the portcullis of the gate.

Chinese rifle sharpshooters spilled out as the gate towers and pagodas came crashing down from the gunfire of Reilly's battery. Shells whined down the narrow streets and burst in the barricades blocking them. Reilly's artillerymen rushed their 3.2's down the smoke-filled alleys as the Boxers fled under the guns' menacing muzzles. "Out of the shattered store windows priceless jade, porcelains, rugs, and skins of wild animals, and incredibly beautiful rolls of silk tumbled into the street. But there was no looting or souvenir collecting by Reilly's artillerymen. The 'Old Man' had so ordered, and his orders were obeyed to the letter and in the spirit given. But that didn't apply to flags and banners captured from the enemy who had been firing at us so recently."

Although the British and Indian troops had assaulted Peking as agreed on at the commanders' conference, the American attack had drawn the Chinese and Boxer defenders from the British front. As a result the honor of being the first to reach the legations fell to the British, who entered the Tartar City almost without opposition through the water-gate tunnel under the wall. But there was still a warm welcome for the Fourteenth Infantry and Captain Reilly's Light

Battery F as they marched into the British compound. "Affectionate cuss words were traded between the hollow-eyed, haggard Marine Legation guards as they greeted with heart-felt handclasps the men who had come all the way from the Philippines to save them. With joyous smiles and misty eyes, it was a heart-warming meeting with the brave missionaries and civilians who had taken their share of guard duty at the barricades and loopholes, and with the exhausted, worn-out, courageous women and frail, skinny children who had prepared the meager meals and operated the hospital facilities and suffered all the hardships of the siege in which sixty-five defenders had been killed and 135 wounded. Down to their last meal of pony meat, the relief had come none too soon.

"The international force had successfully accomplished the first part of its mission—saving their countrymen in the legations, and many Chinese Christians, from certain death or, what was even worse, torture by the fanatical members of the 'Fists of Righteous Harmony' and the Imperial troops. Within the inner rings of the Chinese puzzle, the Imperial City and the Forbidden City, the enemy lurked in great numbers. No withdrawal of allied forces and no occupation of Peking was safe until these enemy forces were defeated and their leaders punished. But for Reilly's Battery the final chapter of its glorious history was about to end—in tragedy."

Early on the morning of August 15 the battery broke park and the center and right platoons were designated to fire from the top of the wall by the Chien gate. The cannoneers prepared the long ramp leading up the wall that had not been used by vehicles for many years. Ten horses were hitched to each piece, with the cannoneers assisting by pushing on the spokes of the wheels. Soon the four guns were on top of the wall pointing westward to the Shun-chin gate a mile away where the Chinese, under cover of the crenellations of the wall, were delivering strong but intermittent infantry and artillery fire. There was a symphony of firing as the battery's guns went into action with the infantry rifles. Characteristically Captain Reilly was exposed to enemy fire as he moved about on the wall to direct the firing and observe the results of the shelling of the Sun-chin gate and the walls of the Forbidden City.

Under the rain of shells stately pagodas and shabby huts alike went up in flames. Seemingly impregnable masonry structures built to endure forever were wrecked under the impact of the steel projectiles. Great clouds of smoke billowed skyward as the aged city of an ancient civilization burned. Peking had been reached and its outer walls breached, but five nations still vied to be the first to enter its innermost holy of holies, the Forbidden City. Behind the race and the clash of arms was the age-old rivalry of European countries seeking trade advantages in China.

As the artillery of the other allies fired shell after shell into the mighty walls, word was circulated among their infantry columns that the wildly storming Americans were going to fight their way into the Forbidden City by making direct frontal attacks through the series of gates. Allied observers gathered to watch the assault—and to see the Americans hurled back. Lieutenant Summerall's platoon had been hitched since early morning waiting for Captain Reilly's orders—while the guns of the other platoons wreaked havoc on the enemy. An infantry orderly galloped up and handed a message to Lieutenant Summerall from the infantry company commander he was to support. No sooner had he read the last word than he shouted his orders, and the platoon set out at a dead run behind him.

Captain Reilly was watching them from the top of the wall. There was young Summerall galloping in the lead, closely followed by four six-horse teams, their manes and tails flying in the breeze, heads tossing, and reins held in the tight grip of the tense drivers. The guns and caissons careened on two wheels as the platoon wheeled around corners in the narrow, winding streets. The cannoneers hung onto their limber and caisson seats with all their might as the platoon rushed forward. Surely Captain Reilly must have been proud of his artillerymen and the battery he had taught and trained as they galloped forward until hidden from his sight.

Circling around in front of the gate of the first wall of the Forbidden City, the teams left two 3.2-inch guns standing out in the clear. Cannoneers flung themselves on the guns to prepare them for firing. Following Captain Reilly's orders, they wore khaki blouses over the more visible Army blue shirts. Bullets from Chinese riflemen peppered the ground around the guns, kicking up little clouds of dust. The gunners, disregarding the enemy fire, from their unprotected positions peered over their sights and elevated the muzzles of their guns with deadly certainty.

Suddenly the allied observers were dumbfounded to see Lieutenant Summerall calmly walk up to the gate and examine the stout eight-inch timbers. Peering through a crack he saw where the heavy cross beams were secured by enormous Chinese locks. Taking a piece of chalk from his pocket, he marked the location of this bar and walked back to his guns. The cannoneers leaped to the trails of the gun and rolled it to a dozen feet from the gate. "Load with thorite," he ordered. The cannoneers handled this previously untried explosive gingerly. Motioning to the gunner, Lieutenant Summerall indicated the chalk mark on the gate.

"Right thar, sir?" asked Gunner Smith of Tennessee as he sighted his guns. "Right there," was the response.

The gun crew stood clear of the piece; the gun roared and rolled back with the force of its recoil. And the gate swung open with a splintering crash and loud creaking from its age-rusty hinges. The Americans were suddenly staring into the Imperial City. The first penetration of China's centuries-old stronghold had been made by U.S. forces.

Enemy fire from the second wall was furious. Although four more walls barred the way, the foreign devils must not be allowed to enter another gate. But the riflemen of the Fourteenth Infantry had moved up on top of the first captured wall and were delivering a hot, effective fire in return. From the archway below, the platoon was raking the top of the second wall as fast as the guns could be loaded and fired. White dust of shattered crenellations again supplanted the smoke of Chinese rifles.

The platoon moved forward to the second wall. Again Lieutenant Summerall carefully marked a white chalk X on the great beams in front of the crossbar. Allied observers watched the pagoda above the gate, half expecting to see a caldron of boiling oil dumped down on his head. He returned to his guns unharmed and Gunner Smith

16. *The Chien Men where Captain Reilly was killed.*

17. Lieutenant McCloskey and "Pet" in the Temple of Agriculture, Peking.

again asked the same question, "Right thar, sir?" and received the same answer. Again a thorite shell was the key to a gate of the Imperial City.

By the same process two more walls were cleared and captured; two more gates were burst open. Lieutenant Summerall's guns were laying on the last barrier, the gate of the Forbidden City, when an orderly arrived with an order halting the capture of the last of Peking's defenses. It seems that immediately after the gate of the second wall was blown open the allied observers were off to spread the word that unless orders were issued to stop the advancing Americans, they would probably enter the Forbidden City not only first but all by themselves. The light artillery of the French, British, Russians, and Japanese was still futilely battering away at the massive masonry walls. As a result of a hastily assembled conference of allied commanders, orders were issued halting the American advance. Five minutes later the gate would have been burst open to admit the American assaulting forces. But "for good diplomatic reasons" the Americans had to wait until the 28th when the allies would make a triumphal procession together into the Forbidden City.

Suddenly Lieutenant Summerall's artillerymen appeared stunned as the platoon stood before the last gate—and it was not because they had been denied the opportunity to burst in the gate of the last wall. It was because a whispered word had been passed forward. Twice a sergeant had murmured to Lieutenant Summerall, "Sir, they say the Captain's been killed." It was credible enough. Captain Reilly had always disregarded danger. But Lieutenant Summerall would not believe it; surely the Captain who had survived four wars unscathed would escape through this fifth one that was so nearly concluded. But the tragic message that reached the platoon as its gun stood smoking before the last gate was true. Taps had sounded for the commander of Light Battery F, Fifth Artillery, as he stood on the wall over the Chien gate at about 8:50 A.M. that August 15th observing the effects of the fire of his guns. He had been struck in the mouth by a Chinese bullet fired from the Imperial City.

"Wounded mortally, he fell unconscious and died in First Sergeant Follinsby's arms. He died as he would have chosen to—with every gun of his splendid battery in action and accomplishing the tasks he had assigned. Captain Reilly was a knightly man with a character so grand, so noble, so loving, that words are unable to express the shock experienced by his friends and comrades at his untimely end. With the battery participating in the funeral, Captain Reilly was buried in the U.S. Legation grounds on August 16.

"To this saga of the service of Reilly's Battery there was another

HEADQUARTERS FIFTH ARTILLERY,

GENERAL ORDERS }
No. 9.

Fort Hamilton, August 22, 1900.

It is the painful duty of the Regimental Commander to announce the death of a gallant officer of the regiment, Captain *Henry J. Reilly*, who was killed in battle in Pekin, China, on the 15th instant, while in command of Light Battery "F" of the regiment.

For nearly thirty-six years Captain *Reilly* has been identified with this regiment. Enlisting in Battery "B" on the 22nd September, 1864, he was promoted Corporal and Sergeant, and on December 1st, 1866, was commissioned Second Lieutenant. He became a First Lieutenant September 18th, 1868, and Captain January 3rd, 1894.

Assigned to the command of Light Battery "F" in August, 1896, Captain *Reilly* commanded the battery throughout the Spanish-American war, participating in the siege of Santiago, and returning to the United States in August 1898. The following April he left, with his battery, for the Philippine Islands, where he did most efficient service, being in action with the enemy there in seven successful engagements. Upon the breaking out of the present trouble with China, *Reilly's* battery was selected to accompany the troops first designated for service in that campaign, and has participated in all the marches and battles of the allied armies which resulted in the capture of Pekin and the relief of the foreign legations.

To those officers of the regiment who knew Captain *Reilly*, no expression of praise or commendation is necessary. To those who have not known or served with him, it need only be said that he was an officer always prompt, zealous, and conscientious in the performance of his duties; a true soldier, leaving us an example of duty well performed by which all may profit.

To his bereaved family is extended most sincere sympathy. Through respect to his memory, the officers of the regiment will wear the usual badge of mourning for thirty days.

By order of COLONEL RODGERS:
WARREN P. NEWCOMB,
Captain, Adjutant 5th Artillery.

OFFICIAL:

[signature: Warren P. Newcomb]
Captain, Adjutant 5th Artillery.

18. *Official announcement of Captain Reilly's death.*

incident of epic finality. Captain Reilly's beautiful horse, which was never ridden again after his death, pined away and died within a few weeks of his master."

Lieutenant McCloskey's letters to the lovely Miss Sara Monro back in Pittsburgh had been almost equally devoted to his love for Captain Reilly and his love for her. She was astounded therefore to read of Captain Reilly's death in the newspapers when she had received no such word from him. A sad letter later answered her questions by saying that the tragedy was too heartbreaking to write about and that he had been unwilling to burden her with his despair and grief. In all his long life he never ceased regretting the loss of this fine man who was his hero and perfect example of all an Army officer should be.

On Sunday, March 24, 1901, a funeral ceremony was conducted for Captain Reilly and six enlisted men who had also been buried in the legation grounds. The battery marched to the legation where seven boxes containing the bodies in caskets were each covered with an American flag. General Chaffee and all his staff and many civilians were present. The chaplain said a prayer, then the boxes were carried out by soldiers and tied on the caissons. The column was formed with four cavalry troopers riding well ahead to clear the street. Captain Thomas Ridgway, who took command of the battery on November 4, 1900, was at the head of the column; then came a troop of cavalry followed by the band and a company of infantry. After them came the caissons, then General Chaffee and his staff. The band played funeral marches, and the column proceeded in very slow time. Lieutenants Summerall and McCloskey rode abreast of the Captain's body; six soldiers marched abreast of the other bodies.

The procession passed down Legation Street and under Chien gate where Captain Reilly was killed. Thousands of Chinese came running from byways and alleys, attracted by the music and the slow march of men. As the procession entered the Temple of Heaven gate, the four walls of the enclosure caught up the sound and filled the air with the stirring, solemn dirge. The cavalry and infantry formed a line in front of headquarters and presented arms as the caissons passed and the band played "Nearer My God to Thee." The bodies were deposited in the quartermaster storehouse.

On April 4, 1901, another funeral procession escorted Captain Reilly's body to the train. Just as the train started, one of the battery's 3.2-inch guns was fired and continued to be fired at one minute intervals until 21 volleys—the national salute—had sounded. Captain Reilly's remains were returned to the United States on the transport *Egbert* for final interment in Arlington National Cemetery

19. Memorial to Captain Reilly, Arlington National Cemetery.
U.S. ARMY PHOTO.

in Washington. He is buried in Section 2, Grave 844. Through contributions collected by the Fifth Artillery in 1901 from those who loved him so well, the grave is marked by a private monument bearing the following inscription:

HENRY J. REILLY

CAPT. 5th U.S. ARTILLERY
BORN SEPT. 24, 1845

KILLED IN ACTION AT
PEKIN, CHINA, AUG. 15, 1900

"I have fought a good fight,
I have finished my course,
I have kept the faith."
II Timothy, 4.7.

There are two footstones at the base of the monument marked simply:

H. J. R.   Frances M. Reilly
                 Wife of
                 Henry J. Reilly
                 1859-1947

On February 13, 1908, six bronze memorial tablets, placed on the walls of the gateway of the Legation Guard of the American Legation at Peking, were dedicated to commemorate the service of the Soldiers, Sailors and Marines of the United States of America in the Relief of the Legation in Peking in 1900. The tablets were unveiled by Colonel Webb C. Hayes, President of the China Battlefield Commission, and accepted by Mr. Fletcher, 1st Secretary and Chargé d'Affaires of the American Legation, and placed in the charge of Captain L.W. Gulick's company of U.S. Marines, the U.S. Legation Guard.

Chapter XII

Epilogue

For several days prior to the arrival of the relief expedition at the walls of Peking, the Manchus had been fleeing from the city in all directions; but the Empress Dowager, Kuang Hsu, and the palace household had delayed their departure until the last possible moment. Outside, the last stubborn Chinese soldier had evaporated from behind the barricades. The time had come, and early on the morning of August 15, Tz'u Hsi gave the orders to leave. She changed her rich clothing for that of a Chinese peasant woman and had her hair style suitably rearranged. Instructing the staff on what to take and what to leave and where to bury the treasures, she was constantly followed by the Pearl Concubine, who implored her to leave Emperor Kuang Hsu in Peking and let her stay to look after him. Finally Tz'u Hsi ran out of patience and ordered her eunuchs to carry the Pearl Concubine from the royal chamber and throw her down a well. At last the procession departed, just moments before the relief expedition entered the Imperial City.

Chinese administration within Peking was nonexistent until the allied commanders divided the city into zones of responsibility, and within those areas they took the measures necessary to establish proper sanitation. There seemed to be no sewage system in Peking, although it was said that formerly there was a good system in some parts of the city. Most of the principal streets had a very high crown with wide, deep ditches on the sides filled with foul water that had turned from green to black. There were no sidewalks and in rainy weather the unpaved streets were almost impassable. Reportedly, it was not rare for men or animals to be drowned in the streets of Peking. Even one of the American wagons almost disappeared from view in a mudhole on the west side of the Imperial City.

All the houses were a single story high and were surrounded by brick walls built as far into the street as possible. Besides the great wall enclosing the Chinese City, Tartar City, the Imperial City, and the Forbidden City, there were minor walls everywhere. Every property was enclosed to form a compound. The doors on the streets all followed the same general rule—there were no knobs, handles, or latches, and it was impossible to enter a compound without the assistance of someone on the inside. The roofs of the buildings were usually of tile, but there appeared to be no system for catching and preserving the rainfall.

Under the direction of the zone commanders the streets were cleared of decaying human and animal corpses. Soon the depressed and dejected Chinese began to come out of hiding, proclaiming that they had always loved foreigners. But when the allied victory parade through the Forbidden City took place, it could hardly be called a successful demonstration, since the majority of the Chinese residents had already left the city.

The next question to be settled by the allies concerned negotiations with the Chinese over the provisions of the peace treaty. But since the Empress Dowager and her court had fled, who would represent the Chinese? The Empress, however, still had a sense of duty. She sent Prince Ch'ing, who had started out on her "tour of inspection" as part of the Imperial party, back to Peking. He was instructed to persuade Li Hung-chang to leave Canton and return to Peking to represent the Throne in dealing with the foreigners. He was to play the old Chinese game of breaking up the allied relationships and setting the countries against one another. Li had been invited to Peking by Tz'u Hsi many times before, but he had successfully evaded the assignment until now. He did not hurry to leave Canton and when he did, he took a whole month just to reach Tientsin. (The joint note of the cooperating powers to the Government of China, signed in Peking on December 22, 1900, is contained in Appendix III.)

Traveling in Peking carts, the Imperial party reached the Summer Palace on August 15, where it was joined by Prince Ch'ing, other princes and dignitaries, and about 2,000 troops. The party did not tarry at the Summer Palace but resumed its tedious trek to the northwest almost immediately. Progress was slow and uncomfortable, and the outriders watched closely for pursuers, who never appeared. Tz'u Hsi continued to wear her peasant disguise and to eat the inferior food of the poverty-stricken, half-starved villagers for several days. Legend has it that her flight is memorialized in North China by a certain kind of bread still served in Peking restaurants. According to the Chinese story, one of Tz'u Hsi's hosts was so ashamed of being able to offer her only cornmeal bread that he put a little meat in one end to ease its meagerness. It is this cornmeal muffin with a little meat in it that allegedly perpetuates the memory of the Empress Dowager in Peking.

But food was not the only hardship suffered by the Imperial party. Sleeping accommodations were another. Some nights the Empress slept on a brick k'ang, or oven-bed that, although warm, was exceedingly hard. In other villages she was forced to sit up all night when no beds were available. On some of these occasions she shared a bench with Kuang Hsu and got what sleep she could—sitting back to back with him despite the fact that she had recently murdered his Pearl Concubine. Their privations and hardships notwithstanding, the Imperial party and the other refugees were surprisingly cheerful.

Conditions improved after they passed beyond the battle-scarred areas. After leaving Kalgan the procession took a long rest at Taiyuan, the capital of Shansi Province. Here the governor was Yu-hsien, the dedicated pro-Boxer. He bitterly regretted the defeat of the Boxers and he told the Empress that he had had every Christian, native and foreign, in the province put to death. The Empress was happy in Taiyuan. Living in the governor's yamen, and wearing the clothes and hair styling of her high position, she presided over many banquets and affairs of state. She probably would have remained there longer but for the false rumors of foreign troops in pursuit. So, at the end of September, the procession took to the road again. Its destination was Sian, about 700 miles from Peking. There the Empress and the Imperial party spent a luxurious year in exile. But as for Governor Yu-hsien, his name led the list of Boxers to be executed under the terms of the peace treaty.

In the late summer of 1901 Li Hung-chang sent word that the Empress should return to Peking, bringing, of course, the symbol of power, Kuang Hsu, the Emperor. When she learned the terms of the proposed peace protocol, she realized that her position would not be changed. Knowing this and the fact that the protocol was yet to be signed, she instructed the party to begin packing. The document was signed in September, and the following month the long procession started back to Peking. While they were on the journey, Li Hung-chang died.

It was a different Empress Tz'u Hsi who returned to Peking. Prepared to be friendly to the representatives of the foreign countries, she made certain that word of her new attitude reached Peking before the Imperial party. During the last part of the journey the party traveled in a special thirty-car train that arrived in the city on January 6, 1902. The "Old Buddha" was delighted with her auspicious reception and the great crowds of welcoming spectators. Splendidly decorated pavilions had been built for her arrival, lacquered thrones and colored chairs had been made to transport the Imperial party back home. Tz'u Hsi's pleasure was enhanced when she learned that her cache of buried treasure had not been found by the looters. Kuang Hsu's position had also improved since his flight from Peking. Certainly he was no longer a prisoner, and when he and the Empress received the foreigners at receptions, they were most polite to each other—at least in public.

Following the Russo-Japanese War (1904-5), the unoccupied part of Manchuria was divided into three provinces under a common viceroy, but each had a governor who was one of Yuan Shis-k'ai's followers. Yuan's standing with the Empress was extremely high, and, although he replaced many Manchu officials with Chinese, Manchu officers were in the majority in the army. When Jung Lu died in 1903, Yuan expanded his military schools program. A military staff college, a noncommissioned officers' training school, and numerous other installations designed to strengthen his military forces were established. In addition, carefully selected military personnel were sent to Japan for further training. Among those selected for attendance at the Japanese military academy was a respectable young Chinese who had joined the army against the wishes of his elders. He graduated from the academy in 1909, and while Yuan probably never heard of him, he was destined to become one of China's great leaders. His name was Chiang Kai-shek.

In 1908 both Kuang Hsu and the Empress suffered from dysentery, a disease common in Peking. During the summer Tz'u Hsi had a slight stroke and for the first time in her life, at 73, she showed her years. Kuang Hsu died on November 14, whether from dysentery or poison is not clear. Tz'u Hsi arose from her sickbed the next morning to name Pu-i, the infant son of Prince Ch'un, as Emperor. His father was to serve as regent, with the concurrence of the Councilors, and she named herself Empress Grand Dowager, leaving her former title to her niece, Kuang Hsu's widow. But that very afternoon she fell into a coma and died.

With the end of the Boxer Rebellion, the Western Powers and Japan agreed, in spite of their natural jealousies and rivalries, to "preserve Chinese territorial and administrative entity" and not to carry the partition of China further, primarily because of pressure by the United States. China, however, was compelled to pay an enormous indemnity of $333,000,000, to amend commercial treaties to the advantage of the foreign nations, and to permit the stationing of foreign troops in Peking. Later, in 1908, the United States used some of its share of the indemnity for scholarships for Chinese students. An era of terror had ended.

In our modern time radicals in China again pose grave threats to the rest of the world; but it is unlikely that Russia, Japan, France, Germany, Italy, Austria, and the United States can or could now come to a multilateral agreement to solve the problem of China, the elaborate machinery of the United Nations notwithstanding. Even Captain Reilly and his Battery F could hardly prevail against the complexities of contemporary warfare and the awesome potential of a Red China armed with nuclear weapons; but the qualities of leadership, dedicated patriotism, and selfless courage he exemplified are still America's greatest bulwark against her enemies and are her real hope of survival. Though a reorganization within the Army changed Light Battery F's designation to Tenth Battery, Field Artillery, long ago on March 20, 1901, and its insignia over golden crossed cannons passed into history, its gallant heritage lives on and will continue to live as long as the red guidons of the Field Artillery of the U.S. Army are flying in the wind.

Appendix I

Proclamation by the Viceroy of Chihli in the Matter of the Issuance of Stringent Prohibitions

On the 21st of February, 1900, the viceroy received the following decree: "The Tsungli Yamen have memorialized us requesting that our commands be issued stringently prohibiting the society called the 'Boxers.' Last year the governor of Shantung telegraphed that in the various districts the society called the 'Fist of Righteous Harmony,' an enemy to Christianity, had been committing trouble everywhere. They had also extended their depredations to the southern part of the province of Chihli. We repeatedly issued our instructions to the viceroy of Chihli and governor of Shantung to dispatch soldiers to prevent these acts of violence and preserve order. This class of society is secretly formed, and the members collect in numbers and create trouble. If stringent measures are not taken to prevent this the ignorant people will become excited with suspicion, which feeling will daily spread and increase and result in serious consequences. It will then be necessary to use armed forces to suppress the evil, and this may lead to serious loss of life. We cannot bear the idea of causing lives to be taken without first admonishing the people.

"Let the viceroy of Chihli and governor of Shantung issue proclamations that this society must be stringently prohibited, so that the people may know that the secret formation of such an organization is in violation of law and that the evil practices of it must positively be gotten rid of and efforts put forth to make the people good. Should those who have been misguided not awake to the sense of their position, and still follow their old ways, they are to be at once severely dealt with, and no leniency whatever will be shown. Both non-Christians and converts are, alike, our subjects, and when cases of litigation arise between them the local authorities must decide them in accordance with justice; they should merely distinguish between the right and the wrong, and not as to whether a person is a

Christian or non-Christian—and not the least partiality is to be shown—thus showing our desire to treat all alike with the same kindness. Let this be known to the viceroy of Chihli and governor of Shantung."

The statutes rigorously prohibit loafers, who have no particular occupation and who style themselves teachers in the practice of the art of boxing and quarterstaff, from teaching these things, or pupils to employ these men and study this art. It is also a violation of law for persons to brandish arms and do acrobatic feats, or to roam about the streets and marketplaces deceiving the people for the purpose of gain. Teachers violating the law in the above respect, after arrest, will be punished with a hundred blows and banished 3,000 li; those who study and practice the art receive one hundred blows and banishment for three years, and on expiration of their terms of banishment they are to be escorted to their homes, and there kept under the strictest restraint. If these persons are harbored in houses, inns, or temples, and their whereabouts not reported, the ti pao, or head wardman, who fails to arrest them will receive eighty blows.

The teaching of boxing and quarterstaff, and for persons to deceive the people for the purpose of gain, are therefore violations of law. Moreover, of late simple and ignorant persons have been deceived and influenced by brigands and outlaws from afar to believe in sorcery, and that the spirits from on high will descend and aid and protect their bodies, so that they can withstand the fire of guns or cannon, and they have therefore secretly formed the society called the "Fist of Righteous Harmony," the members of which have practiced boxing and quarterstaff, which has spread to all quarters, as an enemy of Christianity. This society has created trouble and disturbances, and, on soldiers being dispatched to arrest the evildoers, they have been fierce and aggressive, and even dared to rely on their numbers and resist the soldiers. Such acts show that they have no respect for the law, and, although they have been repeatedly admonished by the civil and military officers, still a great number outwardly agree to abide by the injunctions issued while inwardly they set defiance to the law, obstinately fixed in their decision.

Just reflect for a moment. The converts and non-Christians are alike the subjects of our sovereign, and when differences exist between them these should be laid before the officials for adjustment. But for persons to suddenly congregate in numbers, use weapons, burn and destroy houses, pillage and steal, commit murder, and resist the authority of the officials, such acts are nothing more or less than those that robbers or highwaymen commit.

You people must bear in mind that you all have families living.

Proclamation by the Viceroy of Chihli   185

Why should you allow yourselves to be influenced by banditti and outlaws who excite suspicion in your minds, and you then remain obstinately fixed in a delusion and trample on the laws that will lead to your punishment? Now, besides having sent circular instructions to all the local officers to stringently forbid these lawless acts, and those found guilty to punish them, the viceroy issues this proclamation, so that gentry and people of all classes in the various districts may know that they must not induce people to secretly form societies and practice boxing and quarterstaff, which are acts prohibited by law. For persons to collect together in numbers, and, relying on their strength, to rob and plunder, are acts that the law certainly can not forgive. The local authorities are hereby instructed to arrest and punish those who set up boxing establishments, as well as the leading criminals who excite suspicion in the minds of the common people and thereby create trouble. They must not on any account be allowed to escape the arm of the law. The ignorant and common people who have been induced to join the society and practice boxing should all reform and mend their ways and stop their evil practice. They should make an effort to become good, loyal subjects, attending to their proper duties of life. Those who reform and mend their ways will receive lenient treatment, and their past deeds forgotten, but those who persist in their refusal to repent of their former misdeeds and continue to follow their old course and set up boxing establishments, and for the purpose of gain mislead the minds of the people, these will be arrested by the civil and military authorities and strenuously punished. Not the least leniency will be shown to them.

The non-Christians and converts are both subjects of our sovereign, who treats them all alike with the same kindly feeling without any distinction being made. If cases of litigation arise, these should be decided by the proper authorities. The non-Christians should not act with effrontery and show a feeling of hatred toward the Christians which will lead to trouble. The Christians, on the other hand, should not create trouble by insulting the people and heap up accusations and arrest the attention of the missionaries so as to urge their protection to secure victory in their disputes. The officials must reverently abide by and observe the treaties, and justly and equitably decide the cases that come up, according to their merits, irrespective of Christian or non-Christian alike; must attend to their own affairs and observe the law. They should do away with all ill feelings and be sincere friends. This is the earnest wish of the viceroy.

Let all tremblingly obey and none disobey this special proclamation.

Appendix II

Telegram, Mr. Conger to Mr. Hay

PEKIN, June 3, 1900.
Outside of Pekin murders and persecutions by Boxers increasing. Paotingfu railway temporarily abandoned. Work on Pekin-Hankow line stopped. All foreigners fled. Chinese Government can not or will not suppress. Troops do not attack Boxers. Relations between the factions of imperial advisers very much strained. General situation very critical.

CONGER.

Dispatch, Mr. Conger to Mr. Hay

No. 386 LEGATION OF THE UNITED STATES,
Pekin, China, June 4, 1900. (Received Oct. 24.)

. . . The so-called "Boxers" are increasing, spreading, and instead of contenting themselves with persecuting and murdering native Christians are now threatening the missionaries and attacking other foreigners, particularly those employed on the railways. A well-authenticated report has at this moment come in that an English missionary, Mr. Robinson, has been murdered at Yung Ching, only 40 miles southwest from Pekin, and his colleague, Mr. Norman, held a prisoner. . . .

A strong antiforeign sentiment pervades the country generally. The Boxers, constantly increasing, and now organizing, have the sympathy and support of many officers and men in the army.

The Government is unwilling or unable (probably both) to cope with them. The probability is that if the Government attempted in earnest and by severe measures to suppress or exterminate them it would be met by a formidable rebellion, and as soon as this situation became known in the south other revolutions would spring up and anarchy would prevail. If the Government was strong enough, of course the foreign powers could compel them by various means to restore order and protect. It may be that the only way this fact can be demonstrated is for the several governments to take such combined action as will compel them to either employ the necessary strength or acknowledge their lack of it.

The incidents of the last forty-eight hours indicate quite strongly the approaching necessity of such action.

Every minister here has repeatedly, verbally and by note, insisted upon a restoration of order and the protection of his nationals, and strongly presented the peril to and the responsibility of the Chinese Government in case of failure.

I have the honor to be, etc.

E. H. CONGER.

Appendix III

Joint Note of the Powers

The following English version is the translation agreed upon by the American and British ministers to China of the French text of the note addressed to the government of China, signed by the representatives of the cooperating powers at Pekin, December 22, 1900:

"During the months of May, June, July, and August of the present year, serious disturbances broke out in the northern provinces of China and crimes unprecedented in human history, crimes against the law of nations, against the laws of humanity and against civilization, were committed under peculiarly odious circumstances. The principal of these crimes were the following:

"1. On the 20th of June, His Excellency Baron von Ketteler, German minister, proceeding to the tsungli yamen, was murdered while in the exercise of his official duties by soldiers of the regular army acting under orders of their chiefs.

"2. The same day the foreign legations were attacked and besieged. These attacks continued without intermission until the 14th of August, on which date the arrival of foreign troops put an end to them. These attacks were made by regular troops who joined the Boxers and who obeyed orders of the court, emanating from the Imperial Palace. At the same time the Chinese Government officially declared by its representatives abroad that it guaranteed the security of the legations.

"3. The 11th of June, Mr. Sugiyama, chancellor of the legation of Japan, in the discharge of an official mission, was killed by regulars at the gates of the city. At Pekin and in several provinces foreigners were murdered, tortured, or attacked by Boxers and regular troops, and only owed their safety to their determined resistance. Their establishments were pillaged and destroyed.

"4. Foreign cemeteries, at Pekin especially, were desecrated, the graves opened, the remains scattered abroad.

"These events led the foreign powers to send their troops to China in order to protect the lives of their representatives and their nationals, and to restore order. During their march to Pekin the allied forces met with the resistance of the Chinese armies, and had to overcome it by force. China having recognized her responsibility, expressed her regrets, and manifested the desire to see an end put to the situation created by the disturbances referred to, the powers have decided to accede to her request on the irrevocable conditions enumerated below, which they deem indispensable to expiate the crimes committed and to prevent their recurrence:

"I.

"(A) Dispatch to Berlin of an extaordinary mission, headed by an Imperial Prince, to express the regrets of his Majesty, the Emperor of China, and of the Chinese Government, for the murder of His Excellency, the late Baron von Ketteler, German Minister.

"(B) Erection on the place where the murder was committed of a commemorative monument suitable to the rank of the deceased, bearing an inscription in the Latin, German, and Chinese languages, expressing the regrets of the Emperor of China for the murder.

"II.

"(A) The severest punishment in proportion to their crimes for the persons designated in the Imperial decree of September 25, 1900, and for those whom the representatives of the Powers shall subsequently designate.

"(B) Suspension of all offiical examinations for five years in all the towns where foreigners have been massacred or have been subjected to cruel treatment.

"III.

"Honorable reparation shall be made by the Chinese Government to the Japanese Government for the murder of Mr. Sugiyama, chancellor of the Japanese Legation.

"IV.

"An expiatory monument shall be erected by the Imperial Chinese Government in each of the foreign or international cemeteries which have been desecrated, and in which the graves have been destroyed.

"V.

"Maintenance, under conditions to be settled between the Powers, of the prohibition of the importation of arms, as well as of material used exclusively for the manufacturing of arms and ammunition.

"VI.

"Equitable indemnities for Governments, societies, companies, and private individuals, as well as for Chinese who have suffered during the late events in person or in property in consequence of their being in the service of foreigners. China shall adopt financial measures acceptable to the Powers for the purpose of guaranteeing the payment of said indemnities and the interest and amortization of the loans.

"VII.

"Right for each Power to maintain a permanent guard for its legation and to put the legation quarter in a defensible condition. Chinese shall not have the right to reside in this quarter.

"VIII.

'The Taku and other forts which might impede free communication between Pekin and the sea shall be razed.

"IX.

"Right of military occupation of certain points, to be determined by an understanding between the Powers, for keeping open communication between the capital and the sea.

"X.

"(A) The Chinese Government shall cause to be published during two years in all subprefectures an Imperial decree embodying—

"Perpetual prohibition, under pain of death, of membership in any antiforeign society.

"Enumeration of the punishments which shall have been inflicted on the guilty, together with the suspension of all official examinations in the towns where foreigners have been murdered or have been subjected to cruel treatment.

"(B) An Imperial decree shall be issued and published everywhere in the Empire, declaring that all governors-general, governors, and provincial or local officials shall be responsible for order in their respective jurisdictions, and that whenever fresh antiforeign disturbances or any other treaty infractions occur, which are not forthwith suppressed and the guilty persons punished, they, the said officials, shall be immediately removed and forever prohibited from holding any office or honors.

"XI.

"The Chinese Government will undertake to negotiate the amendments to the treaties of commerce and navigation considered useful by the Powers and upon other subjects connected with commercial relations with the object of facilitating them.

"XII.

"The Chinese Government shall undertake to reform the office of foreign affairs, and to modify the court ceremonial relative to the reception of foreign representatives in the manner which the Powers shall indicate.

"Until the Chinese Government have complied with the above to the satisfaction of the Powers, the undersigned can hold out no expectation that the occupation of Pekin and the province of Chihli by the general forces can be brought to a conclusion.

"Pekin, December 22, 1900.

"For Germany: A. Mumm.
"For Austria-Hungary: M. Czikann.
"For Belgium: Joostens.
"For Spain: B. F. De Cologan.
"For United States of America: E. H. Conger.
"For France: S. Pichon.
"For Great Britain: Ernest Satow.
"For Italy: Salvago Raggi.
"For Japan: T. Nissi.
"For Netherlands: F. M. Knobel.
"For Russia: Michel de Giers."